Establishing Your Identity as a Flirt

Just be yourself . . .

Accentuate the positive. Choose a screen name that describes your best characteristics or most interesting hobbies, and draw people who are attracted to that kind of person.

Create a visible profile. It can be fun to act the Invisible Man or Woman, sneaking from chat room to game site, leaving no trace of your true identity. But offering no hint of your age, background, or even gender, can signal that you've got something to hide (like a spouse and three kids!). Be a little less mysterious and you'll become more accessible.

Depth is in the details. If you are mad for Volkswagen Beetles; have taught yourself to play Mozart on a harmonica; write a little; act a little; travel or dream about traveling—put it in your profile and circulate this info! The idiosyncratic skills, interests, and eccentricities you've accumulated set you apart from the more mundane flirts and make you a real person in a virtual world.

SUSAN RABIN is a relationship therapist, speaker, communications consultant, coach, national speaker, and president of Dynamic Communications, Inc., a company dedicated to "making relationships work." She has appeared on many TV shows, including *Oprah*, *Sally Jessy Raphael*, *Good Morning America*, *Today*, and CNN. She is a frequent guest on radio and has been quoted in newspapers and magazines internationally, including the *New York Times*. Susan is the former Family Living/Sex Education Coordinator for the New York City Board of Education and is the director of the New York City–based School of Flirting®. She is the author of *101 Ways to Flirt* and *How to Attract Anyone, Anytime, Anyplace* (Plume). Susan lives and works in New York City.

BARBARA LAGOWSKI is a former editor and the author of fourteen books.

Also by Susan Rabin

How to Attract Anyone, Anytime, Anyplace:
The Smart Guide to Flirting

101 Ways to Flirt

CYBERFLIRT

How to Attract Anyone, Anywhere on the World Wide Web

Susan Rabin
with Barbara Lagowski

Ⓟ

A PLUME BOOK

PLUME
Published by the Penguin Group
Penguin Putnam Inc., 375 Hudson Street, New York, New York 10014, U.S.A.
Penguin Books Ltd, 27 Wrights Lane, London W8 5TZ, England
Penguin Books Australia Ltd, Ringwood, Victoria, Australia
Penguin Books Canada Ltd, 10 Alcorn Avenue, Toronto, Ontario, Canada M4V 3B2
Penguin Books (N.Z.) Ltd, 182–190 Wairau Road, Auckland 10, New Zealand

Penguin Books Ltd, Registered Offices: Harmondsworth, Middlesex, England

First published by Plume, a member of Penguin Putnam Inc.

First Printing, July, 1999
10 9 8 7 6 5 4 3 2 1

LIBRARY OF CONGRESS CATALOGING-IN-PUBLICATION DATA

Rabin, Susan.
    Cyberflirt : how to attract anyone, anywhere on the World Wide Web / Susan Rabin
with Barbara Lagowski.
        p.   cm.
    Includes bibliographical references and index.
    ISBN 0-452-28054-0
    1. Man–woman relationships. 2. Interpersonal communication. 3. Online chat
groups. 4. Online etiquette. 5. Information superhighway—Social aspects. 6. Internet (Computer network)—Social aspects. I. Lagowski, Barbara. II. Title.
HQ801.R13   1999
306.7'0285—dc21   98-51390
                                                                         CIP

Printed in the United States of America
Set in Futura Book
Designed by Leonard Telesca

This book is dedicated to all my readers who have made my life a great success by letting me make their lives more successful. And to all new readers, may you become whatever you wish and be with whomever you desire.

To family, friends, men in my life and everyone who has touched my life and helped me to grow.

I no longer feel like "the salmon who swam upstream," as I said in the dedication of my first book, *How to Attract Anyone, Anytime, Anyplace*. Thank you all for reversing the current by encompassing the exciting, empowering psychology and philosophy behind the word FLIRTING!

ACKNOWLEDGMENTS

Thanks!

To the readers of *How to Attract Anyone, Anytime, Anyplace* and *101 Ways to Flirt* for sharing your comments and inspiration with me. Your successes are mine and empower me to lecture and write more books.

To Sandra Martin and Lisa Hagen, the best agents and friends a flirt can have.

To Jennifer Moore, my editor, for her assistance and belief.

To Lisa Johnson, publicity, for her ideas and continued support.

To Lynn Reich and Jan Lifshutz, my terrific assistants.

To Barbara Lagowski, writer extraordinaire and my internet buddy.

To Susan Greenberg from Brooklyn, New York, my childhood self, for helping me to keep a playful attitude and have fun flirting, no matter what life challenges Susan Rabin, my adult self, experienced.

To those I have flirted with, and who flirted back. Didn't we have fun?

CONTENTS

CYBERFLIRTATION:
THE NEXT ROMANTIC
FRONTIER

Not long ago, I would have proudly told you that I had flirted in virtually every location accessible to the adventurous flirt by land, sea or air. Indeed, I can report with unabashed pleasure that I have made eye contact on municipal buses from Manhattan to Madrid, broken the ice on the Star Ferry from Kowloon to Hong Kong, enjoyed some mutually satisfying social intercourse (conversation, of course!) down under in Sydney, Australia, and even tried my hand at drive-by flirtation on the congested freeways surrounding Los Angeles. Those of you who have read my previous books, attended my seminars or enrolled in one of my School of Flirting® events know that I have literally made it my business to flirt my way around the world. But around the world just isn't good enough for today's wired-and-ready, technologically informed flirt anymore.

I was first introduced to the World Wide Web a number of years ago, at a conference for women in business. Of the many seminars available, the internet workshop was among the most sparsely attended. But after spending what seemed like the shortest afternoon of my life immersed in this new phenomenon, I could not wait to tap into the internet's potential as a marketing tool. Still, there was no way I could have predicted that this somewhat bewildering, completely overwhelming but utterly fascinating computer innovation would become the next—and perhaps the most fertile—romantic frontier, until I took the plunge and signed-on.

A few clicks and I was hooked. The web, I discovered, wasn't just an information warehouse where I could search for answers. It was the ultimate "mixer" where men and women of all ages and backgrounds could search for *and find* compatible companionship! Nor (contrary to the beliefs of the well-meaning business types who organized the conference I had attended) could the internet be dismissed as a "marketing tool." Cyberspace was wildly social! And the most creative singles I knew were using it to market *themselves*, to develop and promote the characteristics that made them unique and to discover the joys of love à la modem. What real-life singles organization, matchmaking service or nightclub could offer me intercontinental contacts, at-home service and the option to flirt twenty-four hours a day? None! I began spending more and more time surfing the web . . . and less and less time cruising the traditional singles scenes.

Since then the internet has put thousands of new friends, on-line companions and hot romantic prospects quite literally at my fingertips. Along the way, I've met many experienced on-line flirts who shared the insight and information that was instrumental in turning me from a technologically challenged "newbie" to an accomplished, experienced "'net-worker." These include Rich Gosse, founder of American Singles, the world's largest nonprofit singles organization, who brought my School of Flirting® to the West Coast and Australia; Dan Bender who introduced me to a slew of potential suitors by naming me Cupid's Network "Woman of the Month." (Dan is the talented webmaster for American Singles [www.as.org] and Cupid's Network [www.cupidnet.com] and the exuberant 'net-guide who directed me toward some of the web's most interesting singles sites); and the amazingly creative Matthew Mohr at Millennial Web [www.millweb.com] who helped me establish a permanent residence in cyberspace by designing my suc-cessul web page [www.schoolofflirting.com].

As I have learned, cyberflirting is a process that begins in the mind, develops on the screen and, for too many 'netversation-impaired flirts, ends either nowhere or in a "flame." My intention is that this book go beyond the ubiquitous "singles web-guide" for-mat to show you everything you need to know to form dynamic, meaningful and lasting liaisons on the World Wide Web. Filled with true stories culled from the trenches of cybersingledom, this book gives you the communication know-how you'll need to be a standout in your favorite chat room, to write and place personal ads* that attract attention and to use e-mail, message boards or even an evening in the on-line auditorium to add excitement and romance to your netscapades. Most of all, this book features my own secrets for transforming a rather sedate trip down the infor-mation superhighway into an endlessly fascinating, deeply fulfill-ing romantic adventure! In *Cyberflirt*, I show you which flashes of keyboard inspiration can turn you into a dimensional, dashing and utterly unforgettable on-screen personality, the ten conversa-tional openers that never fail to attract interest, how to avoid the common mistakes that make on-line romances crash, where to go and what to do on a virtual date and everything else you need to know to make the connection of a lifetime.

Are you ready to trade in your singles clubs memberships and stash of Club Med "poppit" beads for a close encounter of the 'net kind? Why not? If you are logged on with an internet server, you may be within a few keystrokes of the relationship of your dreams! This book can make your fantasies of love with the virtually perfect stranger come alive.

Happy cyberflirting!

---

*The screen names used in this book are the creations of the authors and appear here for illustrative purposes only. If you happen to use one of these screen names in the course of your electronic correspondence, I hope that you will consider the consequences.

CYBERFLIRT

1
Yes, You Can Program Romance into Your Netscapades

"I've heard that everybody on the internet is either a sex-starved computer nerd or a scam artist. Is it possible for me to make a meaningful connection on-line?"

"I'm too shy to make it in the singles bars. Won't I be a wallflower in the on-line chat rooms, too?"

"Doesn't the fact that I'm flirting on-line send the message that I'm a social flop who can't meet anyone any other way?"

In January 1997, in preparation for my appearance as a guest host of an upcoming chat about flirting in the 1990s, Prodigy posted a brief but very revealing poll for its users. The results of that poll gave me plenty of fodder for chat. It also convinced me that although I had already written two successful books on the joys of flirting, *How to Attract Anyone, Anytime, Anyplace* and *101 Ways to Flirt*, although my "School of Flirting®" had made news from the Upper West Side of Manhattan to the land Down Under, and although I had personally trained thousands of master flirts, many of whom had met their matches and retired from the singles scene, I still had my work cut out for me. For when the Prodigy flirts were asked whether they "worry that making the first move would make them seem too aggressive," 53 percent of them answered yes. When asked whether they were concerned that they would say the wrong thing and look stupid, 61 percent answered in the affirmative. And when asked whether they were worried that others would not find them attractive, a whopping 64 percent responded that their perception of their looks sometimes held them back.

Since the publication of my first book, I have received letters from countless flirts of all ages and nationalities. Many of them were converts to flirting à la Rabin. They had come to understand that social intercourse—or conversation—can be better than sex (for one thing, you can do it anywhere!), that "flirt" is not a five-letter synonym for all those four-letter words meaning "tease" and that flirting is neither insincere nor manipulative but an honest and charming expression of interest in another person. In other words, the flirts who wrote to me had changed their thinking and consequently their lives. But apparently the Prodigy flirts had not heard the news. It disturbed me that they were so fearful of saying the wrong thing that, in the end, they said nothing at all. It disappointed me that, certain they would be rejected, they effectively rejected themselves before anyone could do it for them. But what shocked and amazed me most was that these on-line flirts were revealing their flirting challenges on the very media that could eradicate them!

The risks involved in making an impression in an appearance-obsessed world and the embarrassment of face-to-face rejection are perils that don't affect the cyberflirt—and this is only the beginning! Flirting on-line frees you from a host of off-line pitfalls, including shyness (there are literally dozens of ways to introduce yourself to someone, none of them face to face), incompatability (poof! Mr./Ms. Wrong is gone. Just like that!) and geographic limitations (stuck in a small town? Not anymore). And if you do happen to say the wrong thing? No problem! Excuse yourself briefly then reappear under a new screen name, one that is more apt to conjure up your most charming self. And that's only a handful of the reasons 'net surfers everywhere are riding the newest wave in flirtation.

WHAT ELSE HAS CLUB MODEM GOT THAT OTHER SINGLES JOINTS HAVE NOT?

Are today's eligible men and women really ready to trade in their singles club memberships and stash of Club Med "poppit beads" for a close encounter of the 'net kind? The fact is, millions of them already have! It is estimated that more than 62 million users are on-line in the U.S. alone, and it is believed that an additional one million new subscribers ("newbies") sign-on to various internet services each week. Since the most frequently visited websites continue to be those that deal with love, sex and personal interaction (the average web user is in his or her thirties so you know what's on their minds!), it is clear that this enormous and constantly growing group is not looking for CNN's take on the late-breaking news but for an innovative way to break into a new partnership.

And for that, the World Wide Web is a universe without parallel. These are just a few of the benefits of looking for love in all the web places:

• There are virtually unlimited numbers of prospective partners. It may be possible to work your way through the available men or women in your hometown—even if you broaden your search to include everyone whose age falls somewhere between the developement of twelve-year molars and the need for dentures. But with the equivalent of a city's worth of newbies settling into the internet community every day, you'll never run out of possibilities!

• There is flirtation without barriers. Who among us hasn't wished there was a gathering place where singles could mix and mingle free of the visuals that subject us to ageism, sexism and ethnic or cultural stereotyping? I know I have, but I don't anymore! The internet has been my link to hundreds of fascinating and diverse people I would never have otherwise encountered—not even in my hometown of Manhattan. The internet is *the* place to be for any flirt who is frustrated by a reach that does not exceed his or her grasp.

• Flirting has been transformed into a twenty-four-hour-a-day proposition! I understand that some eligible men and women prefer shut-eye to open dialogue in the wee hours, but I've met some rather dreamy night owls at 3 a.m. It beats reading a dull book and hoping to fall back to sleep.

• It's a setting for romance that is as limitless as your imagination, yet entirely within your control. Flirting isn't just about bars anymore. It's about a virtually boundless menu of options you can tailor to suit your own personal needs, desires and preferences! Tired of trying to converse in a noisy disco? You'll find a chat room that's just jazzy enough for you. Prefer to pick up information and new friends in an educational setting? Try an informational auditorium. (Learn while you yearn!) If you're looking for a significant other who shares your profession, hobby or personal predilection, check the message boards. It's likely your dream date is there.

And if you simply prefer that your romances be romantic? You've come to the right place. The rousing, randy e-mail reverie is the twenty-first-century equivalent of the heart-stirring billet-doux. And that's what makes electronic correspondence a great option for flirts who prefer their computers fast but their courtships tantalizingly slow.

• Most of all, the internet draws out some of the most elusive and charming types of flirts: those who are quiet, a tad insecure, or fearful of face-to-face encounters! If you are a shy flirt, one of the chronically tongue-tied, a strong-and-silent type or simply one of those very witty men and women who know exactly the right thing to say ten minutes after the opportunity to say it has gone, you'll find a home here. Chat rooms and message boards allow you to collect your thoughts, consider your answers and be glib at your own pace. Your unique personality will shine—and you'll develop a sense of confidence that will carry over into your real-life encounters.

As for the many flirts who have come to feel overlooked, devalued or simply underutilized, you'll find an appreciative audience on the internet! Older women, clear your e-mail boxes! You may be hearing from many more younger men than you ever dreamed. (I have hats that are older than the men who have courted me on the web!) As for you busy professionals who believe that a seventy-hour work week doesn't leave time for romance . . . guess again! I've made contact with up to twenty potential paramours in a single lunch hour (and with chopsticks in one hand!).

Cyberflirtation can be whatever you choose to make it: a route to friendship, an inroad to an intimate relationship, the basis of a meaningful romance, a professional resource (remember: Flirting isn't about sex; it's about communication) or a cross-cultural awakening. And other than a slight case of eye strain or perhaps carpal tunnel syndrome, it is entirely without physical superficialities, dress code, or hazard, as long as you consider the realities of meeting a broad cross-section of humanity, each with his or her unpredictable predilections and motivations.

FLIRTING WITHOUT DISASTER

News stories abound about the "dark side of the internet." Abduction, sexual and physical abuse, fraud, murder . . . this is the stuff gripping headlines are made of. Fortunately these crimes and the people who commit them aren't a part of most internet flirts' lives. And they aren't likely to become a part of yours.

While I would never diminish the experiences of men and women who have encountered such problems, I have met many more whose lives were terribly damaged by real-world dating dilemmas. Certainly factors like questionable judgment, unclear limits and a partner you don't yet know well can lead you into trouble whether you are making time on Main Street or by modem.

On the whole, however, I find that flirting on the internet allows me some very real protections I do not enjoy when I am diddling about in the real world. At my computer, I am always on my own turf. If I decide that I don't like where I am or the company around me, I can change locations in a matter of seconds. In the dimensional world, escape is not within my fingertips. On the 'net, I can obliterate messages I do not wish to hear by pressing a button. In real life, it can be dangerous to "push buttons" around the kind of people who force unwanted messages on others. And if I encounter a cyberjerk or simply a person I choose, for whatever reason, not to endure, I can make him go away in the blink of an eye. If only I could ditch a real-live pain-in-the-anatomy so easily!

Of course, weirdos lurk everywhere and the web is no exception. Common sense dictates that you do everything you can to steer clear of the riff-raff. These are the safety guidelines that work for me:

• Regard your internet aquaintance as exactly what he or she is: a stranger. Assume you know nothing of his or her background, motivation or intentions.

• Keep you personal information to yourself. Many internet dating services and singles sites offer e-mail or even telephone forwarding services. These features make it possible for you to get to know an acquaintance without ever divulging your address, your telephone number, your real last name or even the city in which you live. And whatever you do, don't ever give out your internet password. Even an inexperienced con can use it to gain entry to your most personal data and e-mail.

If an internet friend feels that telephone contact is imperative, I suggest that *you* do the calling. *Get* rather than give out a number. That way you won't be subject to harassment if things don't work out.

• Don't believe what anyone tells you. Everything you know about a 'net-quaintance could be the truth, or it could be a compilation of hand-picked omissions, some easily misconstrued "spin" and total fabrications. When you think about it, you can't even be entirely positive of a 'net friend's gender, can you? And that's pretty basic information.

The web is a very popular destination for those adults who feel the need to "reinvent themselves." Remember: You don't get crushed throwing the bull. You get crushed trying to catch it.

• Don't respond to obscene, hostile or threatening messages. Just ignore them. Most are sent by immature men and women who want to shock you into a response. If they persist, report the smut-meister to his or her server. Most servers will take action immediately.

• Be aware that the internet is not anonymous. Oh sure, you can vent your spleen in a nasty message then run it through an anonymous remailer, but it still leaves a digital trail. If you are reluctant to own up to something you've said, my advice is don't say it at all.

• And use your head if you choose to meet the special someone face to face. What you are planning is a blind date with a total stranger. Agree to meet only in a public place. That means no cars, no secluded spots, no apartments or houses . . . you get my drift. Better yet, don't take that on-line relationship off-line until you've read my guidelines on page 111. It's always better to be safe than sorry.

A NOTE TO THE
TECHNOLOGICALLY CHALLENGED

I was not brought up in the computer age. My idea of a hard drive is a Mack truck. Everything I know about the latest programs is in this week's *TV Guide*. Consequently, this is a book about technique, not technology.

To reassure those of you who, like me, don't even own a pocket protector, here is the one piece of technological information you will need to begin your adventure as a cyberflirt:

You must sign-on with an internet service provider.

On-line services such as America Online, Prodigy, Compuserve, as well as the many independent service providers (ISPs), will provide you with the software necessary to connect you to the internet.

It may also be some relief to learn that there are lots of things you *don't* have to know to launch your romantic quest into cyberspace, most notably how your computer works and how the internet works. To me, these are mysteries that are better left unexplored . . . sort of like the inner workings of a kiss. What gratifies me is the result; it is unlikely that the experience will be heightened by a deeper understanding of the mucous membranes involved.

LOOKING FOR LOVE IN ALL THE WEB PLACES

The internet is an educational, entertaining, endlessly fascinating and relatively secure place to meet that special man or woman—or a few hundred special someones! But hold on to your mouse for a moment. Your romantic sojourn in cyberspace will progress much smoother if you consider these helpful hints:

• According to statistics gathered by the Intelliquest Information Group, the men and women you are most likely to meet on-line are under age 40, educated (43 percent of internet users are college grads) and have an average income of $55,000 (more than twice the national average). I don't know about you, but I'll take those odds.

• The internet is a wonderful place to meet "the keepers" you won't find in the bars. Shy and quiet flirts can really shine here!

• Night owls take note: Socializing doesn't have to end at closing time! Flirting is a round-the-clock proposition on the 'net.

• What goes around in cyberspace comes around. Be aware of the kind of signals you are sending.

• Don't assume too much intimacy. Let your new friends earn your trust over time.

• Don't let a case of technophobia stop you! You can bet that Angie Dickinson didn't stop to check the wiring diagram for the Love Boat before she got on board!

2
What's Your Line On-Line? Identifying Your Internet Flirting Style

"Let me make this much clear: I don't fish in the desert, I don't sunbathe in the shower, and I don't flirt on my computer," insisted Daphne, a 33-year-old fact checker for a national magazine. "The only reason I even own a computer is to make my work easier. If I were interested in meeting new people I would go out on the town, not out on a fiber-optic adventure."

"I understand," I assured her. "To you, the internet is the ultimate library. You are comfortable using it to look up the life span of the tsetse fly or the relative weight of a bag of Doritos on Pluto . . . but you'd never use it to try to locate a long-lost friend or to network with people in your field. Right?"

"Well, I might have done a *little* networking," she admitted, "but only when it was professionally necessary."

"And you've certainly never left a message on a message board or a news service . . ." I prompted.

"Well, I *have* done that. . . ."

"But you've never attended a lecture in an on-line auditorium and chatted among the other men and women in your row. And you've never congratulated some creative stranger on his funny or fascinating homepage. And you've certainly never responded to an instant message from someone you didn't know. . . ."

"Okay, okay, you've got me," Daphne laughed. "Although I never really thought of it that way, I *do* flirt on-line. But that raises another issue, doesn't it? I mean, now that I admit I'm flirting, why isn't anyone flirting back?"

I knew that Daphne had been flirting on-line. She *had* to have been. While most of the singles I knew were interested in one thing or another, only she seemed to be curious about almost everything, from the rules of the Scottish sport of "curling" to the types of dogs best suited to apartment life and busy single owners, to the care and repair of state-of-the-art mountain bikes. (Daphne keeps two suspended from her kitchen ceiling.) Curious, adventurous and irrepressibly gregarious, my researcher-friend was the absolute last person who could plunk herself in front of a monitor, surf the 'net for obscure references and multifarious bits of information for up to twelve hours a day and express not a whit of curiosity about the many ways the World Wide Web might change her life.

But that doesn't mean I was surprised to hear Daphne's protests. I have heard them nearly as many times as I have introduced myself as a dedicated and satisfied cyberflirt. The efficient and singlemindedly productive among us (you may be one of those people who believe that using an office Xerox machine to copy anything but work-related materials, including body parts, is theft) would love to believe that we as workers are so lacking in imagination and intellect that we are able to turn off the internet's power as a social tool and concentrate solely on its benefits to our work. But the research tells another story. While it is difficult to determine how many of the 78 million singles in the U.S. are using the web for a major part of their social life, I can say for sure that since its creation in 1995, at least 4 million singles have passed through the cyberdoors of the American Singles (www.as.org) site alone. Since there are literally thousands of singles sites, we can roughly estimate that by the year 2000, at least 25 percent of the singles population will have used the 'net to find love in one way or another. I think it is safe to estimate that the 'net is serving about 20 million singles (and growing), in what can only be called the largest singles gathering ever—namely cyberspace.

The good news for women is: 60 percent of 'net users are men—men are the "tech" sex; men are more likely to place a personal ad; and men are more likely to respond to a personal ad. The good news for men is: Women are using the 'net more and more; women *will* respond to your ad; and even with fewer women, there are still great numbers. In other words, if you are an internet user, the chances are overwhelming that you are already flirting—and the way you are flirting may have a great impact on whether or not others feel compelled to flirt back.

Whether you "work it" or deny it, whether you flaunt it or fight it, there is a flirt in you. And whether that flirt is shy or gregarious, bold or bashful makes itself known to everyone you meet—either on the street or in the essentially limitless virtual neighborhood known as the web. This short quiz will clue you in as to the kind of cyberflirt you are. And because it may uncover some social strengths and weaknesses, it is also the key to becoming the best flirt you can possibly be! So turn off the monitor (momentarily!) and grab a pencil. What you learn about yourself and the way you relate to others may surprise you.

1. In the middle of a hot game of "Peloponnesian War Trivia," you are interrupted by an unexpected instant message from someone you don't know. The message is a friendly, but unsolicited, hello. You

a) shut down your curiosity and your computer *immediately*. This must be one of those internet creeps you've heard so much about! If you get involved, you're sure to become tomorrow's tabloid headline.

b) compose a wild and witty, perhaps slightly out-of-character, response. It takes thought and effort to capture a new friend's interest.

c) check to see if you can find a profile for this interesting stranger. Is she (he) listed in your server's directory? Can you learn anything about her (him) without actually getting involved in a conversation?

d) return the greeting and ask where your correspondent lives. It doesn't hurt to be friendly.

e) react with surprise. You're usually so busy *sending* instant messages to "hot prospects" that you rarely get them.

f) ignore it. Do these people think you have nothing better to do than schmooze? Why, there's a universe of information to be conquered!

g) quickly type in a cheerful, "Herlo from Cloveland!" What you lack in accuracy at the keyboard you more than make up for in enthusiasm.

2. You are in a chat room. In the middle of the conversation, a chat participant asks for a "sex/age/location check." You

a) can't believe anyone would even ask these personal questions! Reveal your *age* . . . and your **location**? In a chat room? Never! If you were interested in exposing yourself to potential predators you'd simply drench yourself in meat tenderizer and leap into the lion's cage at the local zoo.

b) boldly announce that you are a 22-year-old from Monte Carlo. Truth is relative. Why not choose a "truth" others can relate to?

c) wait and see how everyone else responds before you answer. You don't want to be the chat room geriatric case, do you?

d) state the facts just as they are, then list all the interesting places you've lived. Okay, so you're not 18 any longer, but you're incredibly interesting.

e) wait until the first person responds whose age and sex matches that of the girl (guy) of your dreams, then fire off an instant message. Why waste time on all these other losers when what you really want has just been handed to you on a platter?

f) don't answer. Really, you're just here to observe.

g) say it loud: You're an f/34/from Valtimore, and you're proud! Oops . . . make that 24 . . . from Baltimore. . . .

3. Your favorite conversational opener is:

a) "Why don't you have a profile? Only perverts don't have profiles."

b) "I'm not surfing for myself. I'm surfing for a vision-impaired friend. I find that I feel best about myself when I take the time to use my talents and abilities to help others."

c) You don't do "conversational openers." Why can't someone else make the first move?

d) "I'm sorry if I seem to be butting in to your chat, but you seem to know so much about the weather there in Omaha. Are you a meteorologist?"

e) "Hey, sweet thing—what are you wearing right now?"

f) I never start conversations with complete strangers.

g) "You seem like a lice person. Wod you mind if i added you to my duddy list?"

4. I chose the screen name I did because

a) ArmdnRedy made me sound like an FBI agent. If you maintain a somewhat militaristic presence on-line you're less likely to attract all the freaks.

b) I knew the chicks (guys) would really go for a name like Big-BuxDan (BuxMAnn).

c) my name is Tim. I was born in Athens, Georgia. I don't live there now or anything; my family moved to Atlanta when I was three. But my favorite Shakespeare play has always been *Timon of Athens*. That's a real coincidence, isn't it? I mean, nobody really likes *Timon of Athens*, do they? Ask most people and they say they prefer *Hamlet* or *King Lear*. . . . Anyway, I chose the name Bettr-Daze because of the line, "We have seen better days."

d) of my hobby. I love to surf—in the water, I mean—and my ideal man (woman) does, too, so HangTen seemed to be the perfect choice.

e) I chose the name HotStuff for reasons that are obvious to everybody.

f) my given name is GSmith but that was already taken so I went wild and chose GSmith1234 instead.

g) actually, I meant to take the name InMaHogg because I live in Massachusetts and I have a Harley motorcycle and sometimes Harleys are called "hogs" but I must have made a typo because it came out ImaHogg. I decided to keep it anyhow.

5. When I showed my best friend the personals ad I wrote for an on-line singles site, she (he) described it in one word:

a) Nonexistent. I'd rather die than write one. If I wanted to hear from millions of complete strangers, I should just post my phone number on a billboard outside the Lincoln Tunnel. Sure, one of them might rob me at gunpoint, but at least that way I might attract someone who'd clean my windshield.

b) Optimistic. Okay, so I didn't exactly win the Mr. (Ms.) Universe title for 1995, but ten minutes every other week on the treadmill must count for something. And maybe the "expansive deck" I watch those "romantic sunsets" from isn't *entirely* mine. (It's mine—and eleven other people's—every third weekend from July until Labor Day.) I *am* a professional (well, at least am a really good billiards player), I *am* available (or at least I will be next month) and I *am* looking (for a good time).

c) Marathon-length. I don't want people to assume that just because I am placing a personal ad that I am professionally or socially inept in any way. So I've enclosed a brief overview of my life thus far, along with my curriculum vitae, a list of my patents pending and a letter of recommendation from my last significant other. On second thought, just forget it. I'm deleting the whole shebang.

d) Totally me! Okay, that's two words. But my personal ad sounds like me: just long enough, just "meaty" enough, just attractive enough (I'm neither Pamela nor Richard Dean Anderson . . . and that suits me just fine!) and, most of all, just adventurous enough to place a personal ad.

e) Direct. I'm looking for a babe. Others need not apply.

f) Marketing. My personal ad would look a lot like my website, which is an advertisement for my professional services. (I'm a CPA.)

g) Challenging. It reads: "SWN (wait . . . make that an M) seeks shrill-seeker (I mean, *thrill*-seeker) to share long talks, rood music, gappy times." (Oh, forget it.)

6. The idea of meeting an on-line friend face to face makes me feel

a) like there really must be a sucker born every minute. You don't have enough problems with lengthy downloads, cranky chat hosts and getting kicked off-line by your server; you have to bring some kook into the mix, too?

b) like getting my hair dyed, investing in liposuction and boning up on the cello. S/he thinks I'm a 29-year-old swimsuit model and musical prodigy who gave up a brilliant career so my old college friend, Yo-Yo Ma, could have an unobstructed shot at stardom.

c) unsure. I'd have to give that possibility some thought until I felt sure I knew what my on-line friend was *really* like. Then, if we still seemed simpatico, I'd set up a meeting.

d) confident. I've had first dates with lots of people, including some blind dates with men (women) I didn't know at all! Why would I hesitate to get to know someone I've spent time with, chatted with or have been e-mail pals with just because we happened to meet on the web?

e) sure that if he (she) is willing and if he (she) passed my cyber-sex test, why not? Ain't nothin' like the real thing, baby!

f) uncomfortable. Flirting in real life is manipulative and tacky. Flirting on the 'net is manipulative and probably deceptive. If this stranger and I had all that much in common, circumstances would have brought us together already . . . and not in virtual reality, either.

g) relieved! You're so much more interesting, humorous, charming and, most of all, *understandable* when you're speaking instead of typing.

This quiz is simple to score. Just circle those answers that most closely represent your responses, then add up how many answers of the same letter you have marked. If most of your choices have been assigned the same letter, your internet flirting style is clear: you will certainly find your on-line flirting style described below. If your answers are split, I suggest that you read each of the appropriate paragraphs. The information you find there will clue you in as to why and how you flirt, and how you can increase the odds that the man or woman of your dreams will flirt back.

The Suspicious Flirt

Other flirts see the internet as a wide-open universe of adventure and possibility. If you answered "a" to most of the questions in this quiz, you view the 'net as a fraud convention. (That would be a "con con," wouldn't it?) Others find the 'net to be socially freeing—a glorious, nonstop mixer where people of all ages, from all cultures and walks of life can, at last, relate. You perceive it as a social club, too—but one that could use a good doorman. Each time you sign on, you are very much aware that you are in the company of anybody and everybody who can scrape together a low monthly service fee. As clubs go, this one is decidedly not exclusive, and you aren't sure you want to be a member.

No mistake about it. The World Wide Web can be a dangerous place. Teeming with people of every physical, psychological and ethical stripe, either acting out or searching for the fulfillment of their fantasies, the web can easily put you in touch with a con. But it is just as easy to find a con at the local watering hole, singles hangout, Laundromat, train station and, yes, even in the most exclusive club in town.

The internet is neither good nor bad. Your experience with it will be what you make it. Right now your suspicions are making it an impossible place to meet others, exchange ideas and perhaps meet that special person who can help you get in touch with the adventurous, playful person you really are. Since you aren't the kind of person who is comfortable taking a plunge into the unknown, I suggest that you ease into internet socializing. If the absence of screening in general chat and singles sites disturbs you, find a chat room, message board or personals site that is geared to one of your personal interests, hobbies or even your vocation instead. This limits your contacts to people who share at least one of your interests and probably some of your values. And for your own sake, promise yourself that you will answer at least a few of the friendly, unsolicited "instant messages" that are sent your way. The sender is assuming you are a nice person. Can't you assume the same until you have reason to believe otherwise? That simple attitude adjustment could change your mind about the men and women who cruise the 'net, and a more open disposition in general just might change your life forever.

The Impostor

If "b" was your answer of choice, you aren't quite yourself on the 'net. Oh, other surfers may be content to describe themselves as middle-aged, a little "mushy" around the middle or just middle-of-the-road. But you're the long-lost cousin of Tsar Nicholas of Russia . . . and a bungee-jumper . . . and you were all set to be Harrison Ford's stunt double in *Air Force One* but you were suddenly summoned into service by the real First Passenger of Air Force One. And you'd love to say more but, so sorry, you've been sworn to secrecy on the subject.

Other women may share the details of their daily lives on the health and fitness message boards. You prefer to reveal the kinds of juicy tidbits that whip the boards into a frenzy! Like what? Like the story of the time the famous physical trainer Radu actually bounced a quarter off your abs. Like the way you simply dropped 32 pounds in three weeks, just by thinking positively! Like the way your life is always just a pinch more compelling, more fabulous, more lemon-fresh than anyone else's could possibly be! Why, just last week you were even a man! At least as far as a certain chat room is concerned.

Of all the types of flirts on the 'net, I always feel saddest when confronted by an Imposter. Why? Because although other singles find them disappointing, frustrating or absolutely infuriating (ask the Suspicious Flirt, above, for a unexpurgated and particularly enlightening opinion of the Imposter), I find most Imposters to be wildly imaginative, endlessly exciting, gregarious, adventurous and bold, with all the makings of a wonderful friend, dynamic partner and electrifying lover except for one thing: the Imposter's need to don a mask and distort his or her true identity in order to reveal his or her most robust and alluring self.

If you are an Imposter, you may think you are fooling someone else, but really you are cheating yourself. By never allowing anyone to know the real you, you foil every opportunity to develop true intimacy. And if you are an Imposter who is also a Cyrano—a deeply poetic and romantic soul who cannot set his soul-stirring words to paper unless they pass through the hands of an alter-ego—you are ensuring that you will never be appreciated for your talents or for yourself.

You may think your "creations" are tremendously inventive and interesting, but the truth is, Imposter, that you are infinitely more complex, fascinating and unique than any character you could possibly create. (Besides, no one reacts well to discovering they've had the wool pulled over their eyes.) So be all that you can be! Come out from behind the false front! There are lots of eligible singles who'll be happy to have you just the way you are: charming, intelligent, vulnerable and *real*.

The Analytical Flirt

If you answered "c" most often, it probably took you a while to pick up a pencil to take the quiz. You see, you're an Analytical Flirt—and as such, you must think everything through before acting. Eventually, you took the quiz (you couldn't resist the opportunity to learn something) but only after you'd weighed the pros and cons and considered all of the possible outcomes. And while he or she who hesitates isn't always lost, it is precisely that tendency—the inclination to look, and look, and look again before you leap—that often leaves you at a loss as an internet flirt.

Opportunity is often like a sunset. Wait too long and the beauty of the moment has passed you by. And so it is with the unexpected "beauties" that cross our paths on the World Wide Web. Is the portrait artist with the wicked sense of humor likely to hang around a dull chat room while you consider and reconsider what might be exactly the right opening quip? He'd rather paint grass growing. And will that gem of a geologist who placed an ad in the on-line personals put her life on hold until you've polished and repolished your response? Absolutely not. She'll be passing the time with some diamond in the rough while you sit at home wondering how you thought yourself out of yet another good time.

A wait-and-see attitude isn't a terrible thing. If the bus doesn't show up on time there is little else to do. But if you're doing more deliberating than dating, ask yourself: Haven't I waited long enough? What if, instead of waiting for the time to be right, I assumed that the time is right right now? What is the worst that could happen to me if, just this once, I acted on impulse rather than using a full-blown plan? And what *could* happen to you? If you kvetch and moan and ponder and never send an e-mail, it's guaranteed you'll get no response. But if you write what's on your mind and don't think your response to death, it's at least possible you'll make a connection!

Romantic chemistry isn't like organic chemistry. There is little logic to the way men and women attract and repel. My advice to you, Mr. or Ms. Analytical, is to turn off the negative chatterbox in your head and turn on the charm. You'll find tips that can help in chapter 8.

The Natural Flirt

You wrote your personal ad exactly forty-five minutes after signing-on to the 'net for the first time. If there's no one else in the chat room, you're perfectly happy to chat with the internet server's spy. You never met a screen name you didn't like. (Okay . . . when push came to shove, you didn't care much for BoyzNBras. Still, the episode was educational, wasn't it?) And last but not least, you answered "d" to nearly every question in this quiz. That's because you're a Natural cyberflirt, and you won't be satisfied until you're experiencing multiple IMs (instant messages)!

Other flirts may not know exactly how you work your magic (although they will certainly learn by the time they finish this book!) but they know *when* they've experienced it. Because a Natural Flirt's focus is external rather than internal, she makes others feel interesting. Because he values other people's talents and abilities, he compliments often, making others feel valued. And because the Natural Flirt understands that flirting is about communication, he keeps every available line open. He approaches and remains approachable. She heaps on the acknowledgment and skimps on the criticism. He maintains high standards without making others feel rejected.

But just because the Natural Flirt oozes charm from every pore doesn't mean there isn't something he or she can learn. Natural Flirts are always picking up and perfecting new techniques. This book will be just what the well-rounded flirt ordered: a foolproof guide for bringing an ages-old skill into the electronic age and an easy-to-follow map for expanding the Natural Flirt's territory from the real world to the reaches of cyberspace.

The Terminator Flirt

Other flirts chat; you commandeer. Other flirts e-mail politely; you instant message and if your IM interrupts, so what? You expect the objects of your affection to stop, drop and roll. Some men and women are assertive. You're the action hero of the World Wide Web!

If the "e" answers were your choices, you have heard yourself characterized as crude, arrogant, leering, thoughtless, brassy, a throwback to an unenlightened century or even as a sexual harasser. In fact, in your long and libidinous history as the Attila the Hun of romance, you have been accused of virtually everything—except, of course, of exhibiting sensitivity. And that is the one skill it is crucial for you to develop if you mean to succeed as a cyberflirt.

Oh, I'm not suggesting that you aren't finding some receptive audience for your provocative lines and sexual innuendo. For every twenty flirts who flee from your overpowering tactics, I'm sure there must be one terminator of the opposite sex who can give as good (or at least as licentiously) as he or she gets. And you are probably getting your fill of cybersex, as well. The question is this: Are you getting what you really want? Many Terminator Flirts are conquistadors on the outside and softies within. If that description rings true for you, if your bulletproof bravado is masking a nagging fear that no one will deem you worthy of an emotional connection, your terminator tactics are sabotaging your chances at lasting happiness.

The men and women I've met on the web are, on the whole, an adventurous, open-minded lot—but they are also extremely wary of sexual predators. Don't pursue, *charm*. And don't push for superficial intimacy, build trust instead. Reveal a bit of the subtle, sentient flirt you really are. Everybody knows you aren't a bad person, Mr. (Ms.) Terminator, so why terminate your chances with bad flirting technique?

The "I-Don't-Flirt" Flirt

"I thought flirting was silly when I was in middle school and I still think flirting is silly now," announced Martina, a 25-year-old bank officer I'd only just met at a lecture.

"So how's your love life?" I asked her.

"Well, I . . . er . . . it's great! It's just that right now it's a little, uh . . ."

Martina's friend Rebecca leaned toward us. "Nonexistent?" she suggested.

"Yeah, that's it." Martina nodded wearily. "Nonexistent."

The bad news is that Martina's love life will probably remain among the missing—as will yours if "f" was your answer of choice—until she loses her negative attitude. The good news is that transforming yourself from an "I-Don't-Flirt" Flirt to an "I-Flirt-on-My-Own-Terms" Flirt isn't difficult, especially on the World Wide Web.

It isn't difficult to become an "I-Don't-Flirt" Flirt. Some flirts of this type are actually shy. Since "in-your-face" flirting is not their style, they brand all manner of encouragement as silly or obnoxious. Other men and women who say they never flirt are stuck in an outmoded mind-set about what flirting is and is not. They associate what is really a friendly, nonsexual, straight-up and honest method of communication with hanky dropping, sexual seduction or other forms of manipulation. Still other "I-Don't-Flirt" Flirts have been disappointed thus far in their attempts to find a significant other. Instead of blaming the wrong man or woman (oh, they're out there, all right!) and moving on, they swear off flirting altogether.

If you have qualified as an "I-Don't-Flirt" Flirt and one of the sketches above describes you, you have come to the right place: the internet! On the web, shy flirts aren't required to be Cassanova on the spot. Free from the pressure of face-to-face confrontation, they are allowed the time they need to collect their thoughts, summon their courage and add an unending supply of fascinating, creative internet companions to their on-line address books. Flirts who fear being tagged as "obvious" bloom in chat rooms and news boards. Let loose in these open, non-judgmental forums, they come to see that there is nothing manipulative about expressing a sincere interest in another person—and that subtly making your availability known can be a boon to you and a gift to others, as well. Most of all, disappointed flirts learn to react to rejection not by becoming "I-Don't-Flirt" Flirts, but by becoming familiar with my favorite four letter word: Next! The internet *is* a community, but it is not a community with a limited population of available men and women, like the town where you live. Tens of thousands of interesting "newbies" sign on every day. So what if a few of the slimier species slip off the hook? There are still plenty of fish in the sea.

I hope you're psyched to start flirting. But if you still need a push to get started, ask yourself these questions: Do you ever feel like reaching out to a potential dating partner? Do you agree that there is nothing manipulative in expressing your regard for another human being? Do you feel you'd have a lot to offer a special someone, if only you knew how to break the ice? If your answer to any of these questions is yes, your prejudice against flirting is keeping you from making what might be the connection of a lifetime. It's time you gave yourself permission to flirt, on your own terms, and in your own way.

If you tended to circle the answer "g," you might be . . .

The Typographically Challenged Flirt

As a child you were among the first to be banned from the spelling bee. You couldn't spell the word "misspell." In high school, your typing teacher was so sure you had ten thumbs, six on one hand and four on the other, that she actually sent you to the nurse to check. I understand and commiserate. But an instant message or e-mail replete with myriad misspellings and typographical and grammatical errors is really quite distracting. For one thing, it sends the message that you aren't particularly concerned about the way you present yourself. (Think about it. A woman sends you an e-mail with so many errors, it appears that she might have typed it with her toes. What do you imagine she looks like? Grace Kelly? Or an escapee from a John Waters film? I rest my case.) For another, it can lead to many misunderstandings. (There is, after all, only a one-letter difference between "charm" and "harm.")

My suggestion to you is that you enroll in a short typing course—just enough to put your skills on par with your sharp wit or personality. Or consider taking a creative writing course. It will strengthen your abilities at the keyboard as well as your way with words.

As you know, Typographically Challenged Flirt, there are certain skills you must work on before you are considered adept. One of them is communication. Practice that and you will be a more successful flirt.

THE TEN CHARACTERISTICS OF HIGHLY EFFECTIVE INTERNET FLIRTS

"Really, Susan, I get asked the strangest questions on the 'net," my friend Gina confided one night over a plate of nachos. "One guy e-mails in response to my personal ad. Does he want to know what I'm like? No! All he wants to know is what I do for a living, like he doesn't want to know me if I'm not self-supporting. Then a guy in a chat room asks me whether I'm 'into fitness.' What does that mean? Does he want to know if I'm a runner? Does he want to know if I can quote the results of my last blood workup, including my lipid levels and good cholesterol count? Or does he just want to know if I am overweight? Of course, my favorite is the guy who instant messages me to say, 'Hi! What are you wearing right now?' " Gina laughed. "What am I supposed to take away from experiences like that? What are singles really looking for on the web? Friends? Mates? A skinny, gainfully employed lady power-lifter in a filmy negligee?"

Good question! What *are* attractive, eligible men and women looking for on the web? I asked some of the singles (ages 18 to 60) who attended some of my recent School of Flirting® seminars. While my casual poll hardly constitutes a scientific sampling, certain answers came up over and over again. This is what they told me.

Men and women who flirt on the World Wide Web are looking for 'net friends with the following characteristics:

1. Nearly everyone I asked put *honesty* at the top of the list. The internet flirts I know have their antennae out for less-than-sincere flirts. At the first sign of contradiction, they're gone. Smart people! It's wonderful to get taken out but not if it means getting taken.

2. Show an interest in them, though the singles I queried didn't put it exactly that way. ("What am I looking for? Why, someone who is interested in me, naturally! Now, enough about the men and women I meet on the web. What do *you* think about me?") They did describe a 'net friend who was concerned for their welfare, who cared enough to keep up the relationship, who e-mailed or arranged to meet for chat-dates often and who seemed interested in the details of their acquaintance's life.

3. They're interesting. This may seem obvious but think about it: The web is an amusement park for adults, filled with entertainment sites, games, virtual tours of foreign lands, information on absolutely any subject, musical interludes, cooking classes . . . you name it, the web's got it. Though you may not have to be much of a jewel to outsparkle the tired band in your local singles hangout, it takes a truly multifaceted person to shine brighter than all the other available internet diversions.

4. Cyberflirts are also looking for men and women who *are intelligent*. The internet is a techie magnet. It's only natural that those drawn to the web are also drawn to people who are quick-witted, perceptive and astute.

5 and 6. It was also important to the singles at my seminar that their net friends be *sexually non-threatening* and that they harbor *no serious intent*. Although, on the face of it, these two entries appear to mean the same thing, they do not. While more women than men defined "serious intent" in sexual terms, men tended to equate serious intent with the desire for a committed relationship.

7. More women than men felt it was important that an internet friend take the time to *establish a friendship*.

8. Both men and women felt it was important to find someone who *shared their interests and values.*

9. Both men and women were impressed by a partner who displayed a *good sense of humor* on-line.

10. Both sexes also looked for partners who seemed to have an active and interesting *real life beyond the computer monitor.*

11. Most of the singles I spoke to wanted to meet partners who were interested in *taking an on-line relationship off-line* to see if it might survive in the real world. Men and women were both unwilling to take a walk straight from the computer to the wedding aisle, with a man or woman they've never met, as talk show couples do.

Again, this is not a poll. This information was not compiled in accordance with any strict social-scientific method. Still, I was able to gather a great deal of information from what these experienced flirts—flirts who had taken a lifetime of real-life social skills with them into the electronic age—told me. And since you're more likely to get what you want if you know what you're looking for, their insight will be helpful to you, too.

Of course, knowing what sort of person might complete your "circuit" is only half the battle. You must also know and understand your own motives for taking your search for Mr. (Ms.) Right on-line. If, for example, you're directionless and lonely, you may find yourself attracting an overwhelming number of control freaks who'd be happy to steer you in their direction. If you feel that all of the excitement has evaporated from your life and you are looking for adventure in uncharted territory, you may find yourself caught up in someone else's bizarre fantasy—or at personal risk. Or if you're unhappily committed to someone else (and many internet flirts are) you may end up in an ill-advised liaison with the first person who offers you a ticket out of your travails, only to discover, as a very close friend of mine recently did, that there really is no "free lunch," on-line or off.

To sum up my point in computerese, it's GIGO, or "garbage in, garbage out." I have already defined flirting as relating playfully and without serious intent. Since working out your emotional issues constitutes serious intent, it is important that you clear away any lingering "baggage" before you embark on your journey.

Begin as you would any adventure. Pinpoint precisely where you are right now and assess how your circumstances are likely to enhance or detract from your experience. Ask yourself: What is your current marital status? Are you single, married, separated, divorced—or a combination of several designations? How ready are you to reach for what you want should you happen across it on the web? Are you available, with no strings attached? Are you involved but unhappy? You may feel more able to put your all into cyberflirting after you've made a clean break. Are you involved and relatively happy? You aren't alone! The web is a popular source for "a bit on the side." Just bear in mind that nonphysical relationships aren't necessarily harmless. Affairs of the heart can skew one's judgment, undermine real-life relationships, and cause tremendous pain. Personally, I feel that you should resolve your differences with your mate and make an honest attempt to get what you need within the bounds of your partnership rather than share your difficulties with a third party. If troubles continue, seek a therapist with credentials, not an unknown on-line advisor.

Now take a final inventory of any further limitations that may block your ability to make a meaningful internet connection. Is there any personal data you are tempted to lie about or hesitant to include in your profile or personal ad? Denial is a sure sign that you're hauling superfluous emotional baggage. You need to take a look at it and, if possible, unload it. Is your flirting type likely to enhance or detract from your experience? The time to make an attitude adjustment is now, before a chat room full of angry men and women decide to light up your life with a barrage of the nasty messages known as "flames."

Finally, consider the type of person you are looking for. Because the 'net will bring you into contact with many more head-turners than you can possibly imagine, I suggest you make a list. Do you want to make a friend who might become more? Or are you looking for a man or woman to fulfill your wildest fantasy? To make a friend you must be a friend, and that means getting real with each other. If you're looking to live out a fantasy you may be adopting a personality that bears no resemblance to your authentic self, and that means there will be little chance for deep feelings to develop. Are you looking for an on-line tryst, or someone who can be a lasting real-life love? Cybersex encounters are over in a matter of minutes but it can take time to find a truly compatible mate. (Though the tips you'll find in chapter 5 will certainly speed the process along!) Warning for fantasy flirters—cyberspace is fertile ground for pretending. Be a little bit of a Doubting Thomas. If you get carried away, you can be led astray.

The internet is big enough, broad enough and accepting enough to truly be all things to all people, especially where romance is concerned. Just work with the unique flirting style that helps you keep your goals in mind, and you'll never feel lost, overlooked or lonely on the 'net again!

CARPAL TUNNEL SYNDROME

. . . isn't just an occupational hazard. If you're an internet flirt, it can be a symptom of your popularity! What can you do to give your e-mail address a "repetitive-use" condition?

- Give yourself permission to flirt! You've listened to your negative chatterbox telling you that flirting isn't ladylike (gentlemanly). Where has it gotten you?
- Use your flirting style to your advantage. Your unique approach makes you one of a kind. Meanwhile, work to perfect those skills that need improvement.
- Do what you must to be a literate, lucid flirt! You don't have to be Stephen King to let your wit, your charm, your humor and your depth illuminate your writing. (Nor would you want to be! Singles have heard enough horror stories!)
- Nearly everyone likes sex but not every man or woman appreciates being made a sex object. Internet flirts are justifiably cautious. Don't be overbearing.
- Have a clear idea of the kind of person you are looking for, otherwise you'll never know when you find him or her!

3
You Don't Have to Be a Newbie

First, let me reassure those of you who would not hesitate to classify yourselves as "technologically challenged": There are a few advantages to being a flirt who is new to the on-line scene (or a newbie). Many chat rooms and message boards (you'll learn more about them in this chapter) attract a fairly loyal and stable group of regulars. The appearance of a strange, new and compelling screen identity in their midst can be as exciting to them as having Cinderella suddenly materialize at what has been a very ho-hum ball. They'll wonder who you are. They'll wonder what common bond might have led each of you to this particular conversational arena. They will wonder whether you are really as fascinating and clever as your screen name makes you seem or whether your brain is more like a pumpkin. Most of all, if they have attended my School of Flirting® or read my books, your new acquaintances will ask you lots of open-ended questions to draw you out and make you feel as comfortable as possible in their company.

And that's not the only benefit to being a newbie. 'Net surfers are, by and large, a helpful bunch. Just type in a query like "FAAK? What is FAAK? I'm a newbie!" and more experienced 'netters will scramble over their keyboards to come to your assistance. Under those circumstances all you have to do to make friends is remember to say thank you.

Still, after an introductory outing or two, you will feel comfortable enough with the surroundings and your 'net server to want to negotiate your own way through the maze of conversational partners available to you on the web. Good for you! Flirting— the endlessly fascinating process of bringing out the best in others and allowing others to experience the best in you—is a skill that makes *everyone* feel good. And flirting in a world without geographical, cultural or physical limitations—a world that exists only on the 'net—will broaden your horizons, boost your confidence and reward you with a list of new friends and partners that will make your on-line address book bulge, *if* you learn the simple rules of civilized electronic interaction accomplished on-line flirts call 'netiquette.

BASIC 'NETIQUETTE

The internet offers the possibility of flirtation without many of the usual limitations (Bad hair day? So what? Nobody in the chat room is likely to point out that you need a trim!) *but not without rules.* It is no coincidence that the most successful flirts I've ever met have also been the most considerate, whether they are interacting face to face or monitor to monitor. Since what constitutes good form on the streets or in singles establishments doesn't always translate to the computer screen, and since your anonymous on-line acquaintances may have *no* compunction about offering constructive (and sometimes destructive!) criticism on your slightest faux pas, I suggest that you read these guidelines carefully before you enter that public forum.

• Keep your voice down. Typing your message in capital letters, even if what you are typing is a friendly, cheerful, enthusiastic hello, is considered yelling. You wouldn't think of screeching a greeting to an interesting stranger in a singles bar or dance, would you? Then don't do it on a message board or in a chat room.

• Go with the flow. The conversational flow, that is. Crashing an ongoing conversation then abruptly steering the subject to one of your choosing is unspeakably rude. Don't be surprised if you are ignored, or worse.

• Don't pull a Cinderella. Abandoning a conversational partner without saying good-bye is a royal slight. The newest prince or princess at the ball may be fascinating, but interest will surely turn to irritation if he or she disappears mid-conversation.

Remember: Flirting isn't only about finding your "one and only." It is about discovering the one who can shake you out of today's doldrums, the one who can offer you a hand in friendship or even just a kind word. Treating others insensitively cheats you out of an opportunity to make a good and lasting impression on those people who might not be marriage material but can enrich your life in so many ways.

It takes very little effort to excuse yourself politely—even if you feel you must fib your way out of a conversation. Remember, web world can be smaller than you think. You might encounter today's on-screen friends tomorrow. When you do they will certainly recall the way you have treated them.

• Keep it clean. Cursing can alienate you from interesting new men and women who would otherwise be available to you. Making obscene references could get you publicly chastized by a chat room host. (A chat room host is an employee of the server whose job it is to maintain chat room standards and facilitate conversation. Being reprimanded by a host in full view of everyone in the chat room is a singularly humiliating experience for most adults.) If you make a habit of obscenity you may be dropped by your internet server.

In short, vulgarity is never impressive. If you're that eager to impress, try the next suggestion.

• Get real. Smart on-line flirts keep their fake-finding antennae activated at all times. That's because so many wishful thinkers, omission-artists and outright deceivers believe that simply because they have paid their server's monthly fee, they are entitled to lie their way to a better body, a less advanced age, a more convenient marital status and even a different gender! It shouldn't surprise you to learn, then, that with chronic fibbers so plentiful, sincerity is a very hot commodity among men and women on-line.

Of course, there is a fine line between being sincere with a cyberfriend and revealing more than anyone might ever want to know. Some details—like the story of your latest hair-plug failure or the saga of your most recent failed psychological evaluation—aren't going to do much to conjure up a positive image of you in an interesting prospect's mind. Just keep your intentions and responses honest while still maintaining an aura of mystery (if not a bit of decorum!) and you will always project your best possible self.

No matter how new you are to the 'net, it won't take you long to notice that some rules that are considered hard and fast in face-to-face conversation are routinely broken in the process of cyberflirtation. Age is not a state secret on the web. In some chat rooms, I've been asked to submit to an "age and sex check" as often as four times in a single hour! Of course, whether the ages offered so readily by my chat room acquaintances actually represent either reality or chronology is another matter altogether.

Nor do any rules about handling inappropriate conversation in a civilized way seem to apply to on-line chat. Of course, there are still those of us who, having been asked some impolite question like what type of undergarments we are wearing or whether we would like to view a virtual stranger's "artistic self-portraits" would respond the same way we would had the question been asked in a real room: by excusing ourselves and escaping the tactless asker. Instead, many on-line singles openly criticize and insult, or barrage, one another with crude and angry messages and e-mails called "flames."

What exactly are flames? They are red-hot messages, to be sure, but they are most assuredly not "hunks of burning love." Flames communicate a profoundly raw and venomous brand of anger that is simply unacceptable in face-to-face conversation. Receiving such a message from a virtual stranger—particularly if you feel you did not provoke it—can be a shocking and frightening experience. A widely distributed flame sent by someone who has even a hint of personal information on you—for instance, where you work, which organizations you belong to, etc.—can be personally or professionally damaging.

As for me, I would think twice before sending *any* message, no matter how acutely deserved, that I would be embarrassed to deliver face to face. There are simply too many potential Mr. Rights on the web for me to waste time and energy berating Mr. Wrong. But if you are tempted to jump into the flaming fray, consider this: Most flames can be traced. Retaliation is common. And sending threatening or repeated missives constitutes harassment. Since jail cells are not wired for internet access, you can expect that incarceration will not enhance your experiences with cyberflirtation.

SOS! AND OTHER HELPFUL ACRONYMS

My friend Sonia is a truly effervescent personality who has flirted her way from Brooklyn to Bali, hitting every singles bar in between. In fact, she has amassed a wide variety of new friends from her travels, collecting them the way other people collect souvenirs. Naturally when I told her that I had gotten my flirting act together and taken it on-line, Sonia was fascinated. She didn't want to hear about this new flirting frontier—she wanted to blaze the trail!

Before I knew it, Sonia was at my desk and exploring her first chat room. But she hadn't been on-line more than a few minutes before she called out to me in frustration.

"ROFL? *What* is ROFL?" She stared at the screen quizzically. "And IMHO . . . what could *that* possibly mean?" She threw up her hands in frustration. "I don't think I'll be meeting anyone on the internet, Susan. These people aren't speaking English, they're speaking gobbledygook!"

I knew just what Sonia meant. When I first logged on, these commonly used acronyms seemed like a secret code—and one not worth breaking. Was it really too much trouble for my new friends to type out their messages, in full, in a language we could both understand? Was a message like "BRBNC" ("Be right back—nature calls!") supposed to make my heart overflow? And when my acquaintance did return to the computer, was meaningful dialogue between us even *possible*?

The truth is there are plenty of singles who don't use these acronyms when they are in chat situations or creating personal ads, but there are a whole lot who do. Knowing the definitions of commonly used abbreviations like these will help you to break the ice with those men and women who have come to adopt these "computerisms" as a second language. Most of all, using and interpreting acronyms will save you a little time so you can get on with the business of flirting. And I am the last person to stand in the way of that intriguing diversion!

What follows is hardly an exhaustive list of abbreviations currently in use. On-line flirts are most creative and constantly coming up with new ones. And many acronyms are particular to certain chat rooms or sites that are organized around some common interest. Still, if you become acquainted with this brief list of the most commonly used chat and message board acronyms, you will never be at a loss for words or appropriate responses, no matter where you choose to flirt on the internet.

You can post these next to your computer for easy reference.

AAMOF	As a Matter of Fact
AFK	Away from Keyboard
ASAP	As Soon as Possible
A/S/C	Age/Sex/Check
A/S/S/C	Age/Sex/State/Check
BAC	By Any Chance
BAK	Back at Keyboard
BBL	Be Back Later
BBS	Be Back Soon
BFN	Bye for Now
<BG>	Big Grin
BRB	Be Right Back
BRBNC	Be Right Back Nature Calls
BTW	By the Way
CUL8R	See You Later

DH/DW	Dear Husband/Dear Wife (alternatively, Da Husband/Wife, or Damned Husband/Wife. Check context.)
FAAK	Falling Asleep at Keyboard
F2F	Face to Face
FWIW	For What It's Worth
FYI	For Your Information
<G>	Grin
GMTA	Great Minds Think Alike
GR8	Great
HLOL	Hysterically Laughing Out Loud
HTH	Hope This Helps
IDK	I Don't Know
IMHO	In My Humble Opinion
IMNSHO	In My Not So Humble Opinion
IRL	In Real Life
ISO	In Search Of
ITA	I Totally Agree
J/K	Just Kidding
KOKO	Keep on Keeping On
LOL	Laughing Out Loud
LOLOL	Laughing Out Loud On-line
LSHMSH	Laughing So Hard My Side Hurts
LTNS	Long Time No See
MYOB	Mind Your Own Business
NRN	No Reply Necessary
OIC	Oh, I See!
OTOH	On the Other Hand
POV	Point of View
ROTF	Rolling on the Floor
ROTFL	Rolling on the Floor Laughing
ROTFLMAO	Rolling on the Floor Laughing My Ass Off
ROTFWTIME	Rolling on the Floor with Tears in My Eyes
. . .___. . .	SOS
SS	So Sorry
TPTB	The Powers that Be
TTFN	Ta-Ta for Now

TTYL	Talk to You Later
WB	Write Back
WBS	Write Back Soon
WPYS	Who Pulled Your String?
WTG	Way to Go

If e-mails are confusing you with shortcuts or if you don't know what a person means, ask politely and with humor and that will help the conversation. If the person is rude or makes you feel stupid, type my favorite four-letter word—NEXT.

EMOTICONS: THE LANGUAGE OF LIKE

First, a joke: How can you tell if you spend too much time on the internet? You have to tip your head to one side to recognize your friends! Don't get it? You will—once you begin using "emoticons" to illuminate, energize and punctuate your on-line conversation.

An emoticon is a very clever drawing made from type or grammatical symbols (colons, brackets, question marks and the like) that, when viewed sideways, expresses or clarifies an emotion. And what is the purpose of the emoticon? At first, I wasn't quite sure.

The first time I had ever seen an emoticon used was in a single parents' chat room. It was right before the winter holidays—a stressful time under the best of circumstances—and the discussion had turned to the subject of children who would be separated from one parent or the other during the holiday season. The conversation, though heartfelt, proceeded in a rather matter of fact way until one woman began to pour out her soul about the son she had not seen in more than ten years. Although we were all visitors (not regulars) in the chat room and hardly knew each other, we became privy to the woman's most private pain. She raged with us at the unfair treatment she had received at the hands of the legal system, and she mourned deeply for the relationship she had lost. Then she ended her missive with :-(—the emoticon for sadness.

At that moment, that particular emotion—and all the rest— seemed silly to me. It seemed to trivialize what were very potent, authentic feelings. I didn't use any emotions for a long time after that, until I decided that doing without emoticons was actually limiting my effectiveness as an internet flirt.

Anyone who knows me knows that I am a total body flirt. That is to say, in real life I use my hands, my vocal inflection, my facial expression and my body language to express my personality, to communicate the way I am feeling and to convey my interest in my conversational partner of the moment. Nor am I the only one who relies on gesture and nonverbal expression to open the lines of communication. Many of the fledgling flirts who have written to me after reading my first book, *How to Attract Anyone, Anytime, Anyplace*, have told me that they have come to rely on the "big three"—eye contact, body language and a dazzling smile—to captivate interesting men and women and turn total strangers into fascinating friends (or lovers). Since screen-to-screen (rather than face-to-face) interaction removes any possibility of non-verbal communication, cyberflirts can find it difficult to fully reveal their personalities, to accurately interpret the signals sent by others and to communicate their interest in an on-screen partner without misinterpretation.

Emoticons are certainly quirky and fun, but how do they work? Just as vocal tones and facial expressions paint pictures of our feelings with sound and movement, emoticons paint pictures of our moods with type. And just as our physical gestures work to clarify and enhance the meaning of our words, emoticons offer a range of typographic "gestures" that can make our messages more interesting, less cryptic and, most of all, a great deal more entertaining.

Can little electronic faces plumb the depths of human emotion? Don't count on it. But do try a few in conversation. You may find that they come as naturally to you as that devastating smile or "come hither" look you've perfected.

:-)	happy
:-(	sad
:-<	forlorn
:-o	surprised
:-O	really surprised

```
:-D        laughing
}:-(       anger (flirts try not to use this one.)
:-/        disgusted or nonplussed
:-P        sticking out your tongue
:-j        tongue in cheek
:-8        talks out of both sides of his/her mouth
;-)        wink
:-,        smirk
:-#        censored
:-x        my lips are sealed
:-*        a kiss
:-x        another kiss
{name here}        a hug (very commonly used)
{{{name here}}}    lots of hugs
:-#)       man with mustache
(\o/)      angel
}:>        devil
P-)        pirate
<:-o       dunce, conehead
:- <       speaks with forked tongue
@:-)       I have curly hair
:-i        I smoke
B-)        I wear glasses
:^)        I've got a great nose
:-B        I have an overbite (You probably won't want to
           share this info in your first e-mail.)
:-{#}      I wear braces
```

If you're frustrated because you can't ask that fabulously funny "e-male" out for a cup of coffee or offer that retiring chat room wallflower a rose, you might try one of these non-fat, thorn-proof alternatives. The following icons are not true emotions (they neither convey nor clarify emotion), but they can certainly brighten a recipient's day—and maybe even result in a face-to-face chat over some steaming java.

```
\_/\_/        drinks for two
(_)? (_)?     coffee for two
```

&&&&&	pretzels
(o)(o)(o)	doughnuts
[: : :] [: : :]	pop tarts
<%)<&)	slices of pepperoni pizza
~<]	a chocolate kiss
^<**>^	a crab
[@}	a fluffy pillow
}}i{{	a butterfly
>^,,^<	a cat
:<3)~	a mouse
<3<3<3	hearts
@—>—>—	a rose

EXPLORING THE TERRAIN

Anyone who has attended my seminars knows that the question I am asked most frequently by singles from 16 to 60 is, "Where is the best place to flirt?" My answer is always the same. The best place to flirt is wherever you happen to be, and the best flirting partner is whomever you happen to meet. And I am happy to report that that advice holds true on the World Wide Web as well.

As long as you aren't limiting yourself to solitary pursuits on the 'net (researching the sources and dispersal of airborne odors can certainly be intriguing to, perhaps, a chemical engineer, but how many eligible singles are likely to share your enthusiasm?) nearly every site you explore offers you some opportunity to connect with others. In fact, informative and/or entertaining internet sites that are also conducive to flirting are as numerous and varied as your own interests and hobbies. If your interests are diverse and far-flung and you are willing to invest a little time researching them on the web, you will invariably encounter an unlimited supply of potential friends and contacts who share your passions. Besides, I've found that getting to know the internet is like getting to know an especially compelling and complex new friend. Both endeavors are best accomplished when you're at your leisure, so you have all the time you need to explore the unique wonders and interesting quirks you'll find.

Still, despite the millions of fascinating internet sites that bring like-minded singles together, there are only a few basic types of meeting places or venues within these sites where men and women actually interact. And since each type of venue has its own benefits and limitations, it can take some experimentation before you find the right kind of forum for your particular brand of charm.

Here, then, is an overview of the types of rooms and forums you might visit to get your feet wet as a flirt—and perhaps dive into a long-term relationship with an exciting 'net pal who shares your pastimes and passions.

Chat Rooms. Imagine a singles party to which every available man and woman in the world is invited. Now imagine that, as each of the invitees steps over the threshold into that party, he or she is granted total invisibility so that every meeting, conversation and parting takes place without any awareness of appearance, age, weight, race or any other physical characteristics that can skew our perceptions of others. Sound like utopia? It can be, if you find the right chat room.

Chat rooms come in several types, including public (general interest rooms that anyone can enter and exit at will), special interest rooms (chats created to appeal to a specific segment of the population, for instance "Thirty-somethings," "Single Parents," "Chronic Crafters," etc.), and private chat rooms (rooms to which you and all the rest of the members must be electronically invited). Despite any differences in philosophy or clientele, all chat rooms work the same way: as a chat room guest, you may either address the room as a whole ("Hello, room!") or direct your messages to those specific chat participants you find most interesting. Since all dialogue takes place on a screen in full view of all the chat room participants, other chatters will remark on your comments, and before you know it, conversation (and sometimes complete mayhem) will ensue.

The exchange in chat rooms is immediate; Conversations progress at the speed of the participants' typing. If you are sharing the room with people whose fingers can do the talking at eighty words per minute and you are not digitally dexterous yourself, you may be in trouble! It is also common for several conversations to continue

simultaneously. I sometimes feel I need to develop a split personality just to keep up! For these reasons, chat rooms are best suited
for men and women who think well on their feet, interact easily
with others, and type swiftly! It is important to note, however, that
chat rooms can also be a boon for shy flirts, especially those who
feel "tongue-tied" around strangers. Meeting a new and unknown
person face to face is daunting for nearly everyone, but the
strangers you will encounter in a chat room are of the "no-see-em"
variety—that is, they are potential conversational partners who
are simply unable to give you that unnerving once-over or skewer
you with a glance. It is no surprise that many shy flirts and countless others who are simply tired of the physical scrutiny they are
subjected to in eye-to-eye "chat" situations, find it easier to loosen
up and interact under the comforting cover of anonymity.

For many eligible men and women, chat rooms are to on-line
flirtation what singles clubs are to socializing in the real world.
They provide a friendly, low-pressure atmosphere and attractive
"clubby" backdrop that can be very conducive to meeting, relating and, potentially, mating with the opposite sex. But, as experience will teach you, developing and maintaining a memorable
presence in these crowded cyberspace "attract-aterias" can be a
challenge. (How does one compete with someone whose on-
screen name is "Mr$$$Bags" or "MegaModel"?) Because my
flirts' successes are important to me, I've provided you with every-
thing you need to know to get a leg up on the chat room competi-
tion in chapter 5 of this book.

Auditoriums. Want to add significantly to your knowledge about
a hobby or interest while you hunt for that elusive significant other?
Are you looking for a place where you can initiate conversation
with witty, urbane men or women while you stimulate the perpet-
ual student in you? Look no further than the dozens of internet
auditoriums and on-line classrooms where singles maximize their
potential—and the possibility of meeting their potential mates—
every day.

Just as in real-life seminar rooms, on-line auditoriums are forums
where a variety of experts and authorities speak on an endless ar-
ray of subjects, from grand opera to weight training, from alien
abduction to low-fat cooking. (Is that where rice cakes came

from?) Unlike real-life auditoriums, audience members are encouraged to chat among themselves, generally within the smaller, chat room–sized groupings of people said to be seated within the same auditorium "row."

While it is possible to find yourself seated between a square dancer from West Texas and a mosh pit queen from Long Island at what was billed as a seminar on "contemporary dance," and it is possible to find yourself seated next to absolutely *anyone* at a question-and-answer session on flirting (I know—I've given them!), taking a seat in the on-line auditorium assures you will have proximity to a huge number of men and women who share at least one of your interests. Few chat rooms—or even singles bars—can make that claim. Moreover, because there is no reserved seating in an on-line auditorium, you can choose either to pursue a connection with someone seated nearby or simply change rows until you find more compatible companions.

You will find auditoriums and electronic classrooms in use all over the World Wide Web. Many are sponsored by larger internet servers (in which case you must be a subscriber to attend) while others are held at designated times at special interest sites. Sports sites, for example, play host to an ever-changing lineup of celebrities, which is great to know if you are a fan, or a woman who wants to throw a pass or two at some eligible men.

Personal ads. *"Slim, health-conscious marathoner and pasta-holic desires friendship (and possibly more) with male who shares my passion for running and carbo-loading. High mileage (but not high maintenance!) okay. Respond via e-mail to . . ."*

I happened across this message, which was either written with tongue in cheek or with a bowl of elbows on the table, while browsing the personals board of a popular health and fitness site. Granted, this type of message might not whet *your* appetite, but it goes to show you that hard-charging flirts are always hungry for meaningful companionship, and they are willing to eat up every inch of available personal ad space to find it.

Placing a personal ad on the World Wide Web has all the benefits of publishing a message in a magazine or newspaper— and then some. Since you are paying by the word you can be more expressive. A personal ad is composed in private and, ideally, with careful consideration. Because the process of writing such a personal paragraph requires some reflection, it allows easily flustered flirts all the time they need to convey exactly the message they wish. And since the ad writer decides at which site the ad will be placed, he or she is able to target the message to precisely the audience he or she wishes to reach. And that's not all. Placing a personal ad allows singles to sidestep what shy flirts (and many of the rest of us) report to be their biggest romantic bugaboo—the pressure of the face-to-face encounter. Instead of knocking yourself out trying to impress an impassive new prospect, you just sit back and let your ad do all the work for you, secure in the knowledge that if one reader isn't interested, the next may not be so willing to pass it by.

I've found personal ads to be a very viable milieu for cyber-flirtation. My own personal ads on www.as.org and on cupid-net.com (as Woman of the Month) have generated literally thousands of fascinating responses, launched many friendships and inspired several exciting meetings in cities from coast to coast. I believe that this form of flirtation can work for you as well, particularly if you follow the guidelines I lay out in chapter 7.

Message boards. Please leave a message! That is, if you want to meet a virtually limitless array of the top-notch men and women experienced on-line flirts call "screen gems."

Message boards, which you will find at nearly every special interest or hobby site, function much the same way as personal ads do. You compose a message, either entirely of your own creation or relating to someone else's posted question or comment, then wait for a reply. If the site is a popular one, I guarantee you, you will not have to wait long.

For research purposes (there are some benefits to researching a subject like on-line flirtation, you know) I make it a habit to visit several message boards each day, including one flirting site, one physical fitness exchange and one board sponsored by an association to which I belong. Reading the posts helps me keep abreast of recent developments within my fields of interest. It also allows me to say hello and offer my e-mail address to any eligible men whose on-board comments are particularly intriguing to me.

So how can message boards help alleviate a case of the newbies? By offering the fledgling on-line flirt the freedom to interact without pressure. By virtue of its format, the message board allows a new internet user to make contact with others, yet focus his or her message on a subject other than him- or herself. This characteristic is important to those men and women who are uncomfortable with placing a personal ad because it requires them to focus on themselves—to some extent, at least—as a commodity. In addition, the message board leaves it up to the user to decide whether he or she will post a message (and allow him- or herself to be approached by others) or answer a post (and choose precisely those "boarders" with whom he or she wishes to flirt). As is the case with personal ads, the message board encounter is not a chat situation. There is no immediate exchange of ideas or rapid-fire conversation. Newbies (and those of us who like to consider our responses) have time to compose just the right answers, and to look up any emoticons that are new to us. Some boards are so littered with emoticons they appear, at first glance, to be written in the Cyrillic alphabet!

In short, if you are somewhat timid or new to the on-line social whirl, message boards may be a kinder, gentler place to get started.

Singles sites. No matter where I give a seminar, whether in New York or Hong Kong, there are a number of men and women who enroll not to sharpen their communication skills or enhance their appeal but simply because the seminar will bring them together with other singles who aren't afraid to admit that they want to flirt! This no-bones-about-it, "Hey, Look-at-Me-I'm-Looking!" attitude constitutes both the appeal—and the problem—with many flirting sites on the World Wide Web.

It can feel marvelously freeing to visit a place that exists for the sole purpose of bringing people together. You certainly don't have to guess what the other attendees are doing there. You won't hear "Me? I'm only here to meet a long-lost cousin" at a singles site. And it's usually easier to tell the creeps from the nice guys/gals here than in real life. (Hint: The nice ones don't generally ask what you are wearing in the first thirty seconds after meeting.) Still, there is a level of competition at some carelessly run singles sites that can be daunting for many newbies. And the level of conversation can vary greatly from site to site, sometimes scraping the bottom of the barrel.

Nevertheless, I do recommend that you explore these sites, not because they are more likely to bring you together with your one and only (you are as likely to happen upon him or her in an unofficial *The X-Files* forum), but because they are the unrivaled mecca for one-stop-romantic-shopping convenience. The electronic equivalent of a dozen Jewish matchmakers and a teeming city block of bustling singles clubs, the best singles sites include everything from twenty-four-hour chat rooms to busy auditoriums to fascinating message boards, advice and events calendars to an active and ongoing forum for thousands of attractive personal ads. Moreover, singles sites are so varied and plentiful, you are virtually certain to find one where you can comfortably do your thing, no matter what your thing happens to be. (Please note: I am not asking.)

Where to begin? Start with the best I've found. They are listed in chapter 9.

Getting to know the internet is like getting to know a complex and captivating new man or woman. Unless you explore this unexplored terrain fully, with an open mind and without rushing, you will never know what it has to offer you, and what you can bring to it.

I hope that this book will be your guide to truly knowing those you meet on the World Wide Web, and to knowing yourself better as a flirt and an internet adventurer.

You'll get the process off to the best possible start if you remember these guidelines:

HINTS FOR THE ADVENTUROUS NEWBIE

• Helping a newbie makes others feel good. So spread a little sunshine by announcing your "newbie-ness"—then watch more experienced 'netters climb over their keyboards to give you some pointers.

- Successful flirts are invariably polite flirts, so learn and follow the rules. You wouldn't shout your "how-do-you-dos" in a crowded room, would you? Then don't do it (even unintentionally) in a busy chat site, either. Watch the caps.

- If sex is on your mind, keep it off the screen. Innuendo and suggestive commentary is about getting *your* needs met. You're not flirting unless you're making *others* feel good.

- The web is an exciting new world but remember: You'll never get to know the natives if you don't learn the language. Emoticons may seem like Greek to you, but Greek comes in awfully handy when you're in the middle of Athens.

And finally—

- Reach out and touch someone. Add your two cents' worth to the current events message board! Respond to a fellow rollerblader's personal ad! If your sincere salutation goes nowhere, you may need to pick up some pointers on making a more effective approach. But if your message goes straight to a new friend's heart, you may learn more about internet flirtation than you ever dreamed possible! Write me!

4
How to Be an On-Screen Personality

Businesspeople all over the world knew my friend Reuben as the energetic and street-smart financial officer of a major petroleum company. I knew him as the life of every party he had ever attended. Wildly funny, with a smile as wide as his native state of Texas, I was surprised to hear he had tried cyberflirting with little success. "I don't know what the problem is," he said, shrugging. "All I know is that, for once, I can't blame it on my accent."

I suggested that we visit a chat room simultaneously—he from his home office in Austin and me from my apartment in New York—so I could get a better idea of his on-screen style. But he had barely said hello before I knew precisely what was keeping him from appearing as engaging on-screen as he did in real life.

I instant messaged him immediately. "You don't know what the problem is? Reuben! What's with that name?"

"Crudeman," he answered. "I work for a petroleum company. That makes me an *oil man*, Susan. A *crude* man. Get it?"

I assured him that I "got it" all right, and now *he* was getting it—

ignored, that is—for choosing a name that conjured up an image of uncultured oafishness instead of open approachability. In short, one of my slickest friends had sabotaged his own success as a flirt by inadvertently characterizing himself as crass, unrefined and downright oily. Reuben is not the only one. In my travels through every kind of internet meet-and-greet singles locale, I have encountered countless singles whose on-screen names send a message that is either too vague ("Me#000"), too overt ("Hotchik"), too frightening ("Killrboy") or just plain confusing ("Pansylovr"). Even the inexplicably popular screen name "User"—generally followed by an unmemorable litany of numbers—carries connotations of manipulation and deceit.

Remember: You can't flash a smile or even your wallet to make an impression on the World Wide Web. But you can use a thoughtfully chosen and imaginative name and an attractively revealing profile to paint a clear and vivid picture of the face you wish to show to everyone you will meet on the 'net. Since first impressions do last, it is best that that face be friendly, non-threatening, vivacious and playful.

WHAT'S IN A NAME?

You can't judge a book by its cover, but ask any bookseller and he or she will tell you: More than one great book has been passed by in the bookstore simply because of what it was titled. What you choose to call yourself could determine whether you will stay on the proverbial shelf or become that romantic blockbuster other flirts find impossible to put down!

No matter which internet server you choose, you will be offered the option to reserve several screen names that you may use—and switch between—at will. I suggest that you choose one fairly straightforward or traditional name, i.e., BeanCountr if you are an accountant, NoStrks if you are a window washer or some derivation of your real name, to use for business or research purposes. (How seriously would you take a piece of business correspondence from someone who signs off as "PuddyTat"?) Choose at least one additional name you can reserve purely for flirting.

Ideally, your flirting name will communicate a little something titillating about yourself while enabling you to retain your anonymity.

This list of do's and don'ts may help you to choose a name that
projects the best possible image, and can make for some very exciting flirting.

Do . . .

• Select a name that alludes to your interests, profession or
hobbies. Whether your interest is skateboarding (Hotwheelz)
or gardening (Diggingin), whether you are a professional chef
(Spicegirl) or an amateur astronomer (ICStarz), it is a great idea
to broadcast your favorite pastimes. That way those who share
them can respond secure in the knowledge that they've reached a
kindred spirit.

• Consider a name that highlights your most appealing physical characteristics. It is impossible to predict the course of an electronic relationship. But I can guarantee this: Very early on, you
will be asked for a brief description of yourself. By incorporating
some reference to the features that make you unique, e.g., Pepi-
Blond, BrnEyez, you capture the attention of those who find your
particular physical type especially tempting. (Is this attitude shal-
low? Sure! But how many of us can truly claim to be above it?)
Including a clue or two as to your physical attributes also provides
some reassurance to those visual types who have difficulty relating to others in a world without smiles, body language or other
visual aids.

• Ask your friends to check your screen name for any off-color
references you might not realize are there. My friend Marnie suf-
fers from rheumatoid arthritis. Since popping into a dance club or
joining a hiking club is out of the question for her, the internet is
her connection to the world and to a universe of new and interesting people. Shortly after signing on, however, Marnie began to
receive a mountain of salacious unsolicited mail. It didn't take
us long to discover why. Though Marnie hadn't realized it, the
name she had chosen—"BadJoint"—referred not only to her illness but to a prominent feature of male anatomy. Running her racy
moniker past her chums would have saved her the time she spent

returning all that unwanted correspondence, and a great deal of aggravation.

• Rest assured that the hottest names are like the most eligible singles: The best ones aren't necessarily taken! If you submit the name your heart is set on (say, GrtDancr), then learn from your server (who has approval in these matters) that it has already been taken, don't despair! Just add a few numbers or a catchy combination of numbers and letters (for example, GrtDancr4U) and you'll make that popular name your own.

• Think about the numbers that appear in your name. A 73 tacked on to the end of your screen name could refer to your year of birth—or to your age! Do you really want to expose yourself to ageism when you're flirting in the only happy hunting ground where age doesn't necessarily matter? If you are compelled, try saying over 20, 30 or under 40, 50. Or use double digits that can't be misinterpreted (e.g., 10, 11, 99).

Cyberflirts who are left to interpret mysterious numbers almost invariably err on the side of "chronological desirability." Unless it is important to you that you limit your chats to other flirts your age, I suggest that you eliminate any possibility of pigeonholing yourself as "just a kid," "a baby-boomer" or a "golden ager."

Don't . . .

• Become a number! Can you tell me the social security numbers of your ten closest friends? Of course you can't. That's because, for most of us, a long string of numbers is simply impossible and pointless to recollect. If you use numbers, keep them short and give them a rhyme or rhythm connection (e.g., 1999, 2020, 1492).

The fact is, Mr. or Ms. Right can't call you (okay, so it's e-mail . . . so sue me) if they can't remember *what* to call you! So choose a name, select an acronym, anything—just don't choose numbers as your on-screen name or you will become a cipher rather than the one-in-a-million personality so many single men and women are searching for.

• Use XXXs to fill in any space remaining after your name, unless you want others to assume you have earned a triple- or quadruple-X rating. When I learned that the first on-screen name I selected was already in use, I differentiated my "handle" by adding on several Xs. All was well until one day, in a chat room, when all of the chatters were simultaneously sent an e-mail solicitation for an on-line phone sex service. My new acquaintances took one look at my name and immediately suspected that the smarmy ad had been sent by me! It took some talking to convince them otherwise, but I still received several nasty "flames" the next day. I changed my name immediately.

• Be too cryptic. The minute I caught a glimpse of the name "Bozonose" listed on a music message board, I knew that the name had been pulled from the script of a comedy album, *Firesign Theater*, that had been popular on college campuses in the 1970s. How many others would have known that?

It doesn't matter what nature of ephemera you lift your name from—the model names of pre-1965 SAABS, Grateful Dead trivia, common synchronized swimming moves—chances are that the people who do not "get" your cryptic references are people who won't be approaching you. And since successful flirting is and always has been a numbers game, it makes little sense to limit your appeal to a select few who recognize such obscure cultural icons.

• Confuse "hot" with smutty. Allow me to clarify: A hot name is one that excites interest, stimulates curiosity and invites conversation. A smutty name is one that excites unhealthy interest, stimulates glandular hyperactivity and invites e-mail you would be embarrassed to have your mother or your children read. Got it? I know you do!

By the way, the "choose a name that highlights your most appealing physical characteristic" rule does not apply to those characteristics that must, by law, be covered when strolling the produce aisle in the grocery store. Advertising your private parts may generate a great deal of interest but not the kind that makes for sincere flirtation.

• Be defined by your illnesses, weaknesses, or strange penchants. Remember my friend Marnie? Because she regarded her experience with rheumatoid arthritis as transformational and, to a great extent, positive, it was important to her to choose a name

that reflected her reality as a rheumatoid sufferer. And I under-
stood her reasoning. Nevertheless, I advised Marnie not to adopt
her diagnosis as her identity, particularly when cyberflirting. Remember, don't tell all in the first exchange, and never tell the nega-
tives up front.

You know the old joke about not wanting to ask someone how
they are because they might actually tell you? Well, in terms of
choosing and broadcasting an image on the World Wide Web,
it's no joke. Making an illness that is only a part of your life your
on-screen identity gives others the impression that you are obsessed with your condition. Who would dare start a conversation
with you if all he or she could anticipate hearing about was your
swollen ankles, your blurry vision or your tender gums? Not only
that, defining yourself by your illnesses, weaknesses or unusual
penchants sends the message that you might be too sick, too tired
or just too weird for a full-fledged romance. What can your more
robust friends do under those circumstances but avoid you like the
plague?

In short, make sure you choose a name that will give your social
life a shot in the arm—not last rites.

Unless your parents experienced some sort of an epiphany in
the sixties, your mom and dad never asked you what you wanted
to be called. They simply couldn't have known that the little girl
they named Edith or the baby boy they dubbed Howard would
one day feel more comfortable answering to a bubbly on-screen
name like Laffeteria or the rather more elemental KingaConga.

Isn't choosing exactly the name you want to live with—and live
up to—one of the most exciting and freeing aspects of becoming a
part of the World Wide Web? For many of the singles I know, it
certainly is. With a new name and a fresh outlook, they feel they
can be the outgoing, confident men and women they have always
wanted to be. Most of all, wrapped in an identity entirely of their
own choosing, they feel that they can at last become the imaginative and even outrageous flirts they have always known they were,
but were too shy or self-conscious to become in the real world.

If you are still struggling to christen yourself (What, you think
Rome was named in a day? Well, maybe it was . . . but you don't

have to be!), I suggest that you reread the self-examination paragraph at the end of chapter 2. It will remind you of the type of relationship you are looking for on-line so you can match your name to your goal. (Hint: Even if you are upfront about your desire for a mate, a name like WddingBellBlus is scary.)

Of course, even the most titillating name ultimately falls flat without some structure and depth behind it. It is important, then, that you add a framework of dimensionality to your on-screen personality before you move beyond your server's safety zone and into the web chat rooms. That process begins not with supplying your on-line prospects with a visual as in real-world singles situations, but by creating a profile that reflects who you are, and the type of man or woman you prefer to attract.

CREATING A HIGH PROFILE

I had just met Justin at a singles club and found him so charming that I invited him to join me at my table. When the bill came at the end of the evening, Justin and I agreed to split it. I handed him cash for my portion but Justin wanted to apply his half to a credit card. (One man's emotional investment is another man's write-off.)

Justin was a beautifully pulled together man but his perfectly polished exterior definitely did not extend to his wallet. It took him some time to shuffle through the accumulated papers to find the card he wanted. When he finally left the table to pay, I noticed that several of his papers had fluttered to the floor. I bent down to pick them up. There, under his chair, was his driver's license.

I can't really explain what happened next except to say that discovering that 2" × 3" cardboard rectangle instantly transformed me from Susan Rabin, flirting maven, to the Heinrich Schliemann of romance, on the dig of a lifetime. Were Justin's eyes really that vivid or were they contact lens–enhanced? Did the age he reported to me match his age according to DMV? Did he wear lifts? I just *had* to know.

Now, I am not a particularly nosy person. Nor do I suffer from a particularly distrustful nature. So why did I scour that license? Simple. Because I—like every other single woman I know—wanted to learn as much as possible about a handsome stranger who had captured my imagination. And what does all of this have to do with flirting on the internet? Everything. 'Net users as a group are even hungrier for information than I was the fateful night that dashing man and his organ donation preferences fell into my hands. Their "need to know" extends from the latest far-flung and highly technical research to lighthearted trivia on every possible subject, from the ridiculous to the sublime. It is a safe bet that such people would also want to know everything possible about those with whom they flirt and relate on the World Wide Web. That's where creating and maintaining an engaging and dynamic personal profile comes in.

A personal profile is the on-line equivalent of the driver's license I found with one very important difference: In addition to the kind of information you would find in a basic thumbnail biography, the profile offers a glimpse into a person's interests, occupation, values, needs and sense of humor. In short, it adds depth and dimension to an internet subscriber who would otherwise exist solely as a name.

Most large servers encourage their members to create profiles. There are also websites—singles sites and those affiliated with specific organizations and associations—that will post profiles for their users' convenience.

Wherever you choose to post your personal data (since a profile works like a billboard along the information superhighway, why not post everywhere you possibly can?) your profile will look something like this:

SCREEN NAME: DriveMeNutz
MEMBER NAME: Suzanne
LOCATION: Seattle, WA
BIRTHDATE: I'm an Aquarius. Beyond that, mind your own
    business!
SEX: Female
MARITAL STATUS: Single
COMPUTER: Outdated
HOBBIES: Snowboarding, skydiving, marathoning and decoy
    carving. Member Roller Coaster Enthusiasts of America

OCCUPATION: limousine driver
PERSONAL QUOTE: I have always had a dread of being a
  passenger in life.—Princess Margrethe of Denmark

"I've been on a witness stand, I've been in a confessional," said Mark, a young man I met at one of my seminars, "but I've never been so daunted by having to tell the truth as I was when I set up my first user profile!" Most singles—particularly the newbies among us—feel the same way. Your profile will only work for you if you approach it with sincerity, communicate something that will set you apart from the crowd and allow the inner you to shine through. Obviously the rules for safe personal disclosure I outlined in chapter 1 apply just as stringently to the material you choose to publish as a part of your personal profile as they do to information you choose to broadcast on every other forum on the internet. Putting your address, phone number or even your full name into the hands of potentially millions of strangers is simply out of the question. But beyond that, you must consider carefully what kind of personal information—and how much—you are comfortable sharing. Personally, I make it a policy not to reveal any more in a profile, in a chat room or on a message board than I would upon first meeting a new acquaintance face to face, which is to say that the exact location of my home, my habits, my more outrageous opinions and my deepest desires remain my secrets. For those more straightforward flirts who eschew such hard and fast rules, I suggest that you provide enough details so the reader can paint an exciting mental picture of the person you are—but not enough so a creative predator can sketch him/herself into the background. Is Suzanne's profile an example of a compelling profile? It is, and it isn't.

Suzanne's profile paints a picture of a very adventurous woman—one who has made absolutely certain that she will never become "a passenger in life." A woman who is bold enough to risk life and limb in pursuit of her interests (roller coasters and snowboarding), she is also self-motivated, health-conscious (she is a marathoner) and artistic (she enjoys decoy carving). The fact that she makes her living as a limousine driver further sets her apart from the crowd—and offers the men she meets plenty of opportunities for conversation. (I am not embarrassed to admit that I, for one, would love hearing about the celebrities who have plopped onto Suzanne's back seat.) On the whole, Suzanne's profile has added fantastic dimension to her on-screen personality, and left us with a very dynamic impression of an irrepressibly bold yet sensitive woman.

So what's the problem? As it happens, I have no quibble with what Suzanne wrote in her profile, but I do have several suggestions to make about what she failed to say about herself and her life. First of all, Suzanne failed to list her age. As we learned in the previous chapter, age is not considered a taboo subject in 'netversation. While no one needs to know your *exact* age (the differences between a 33- and a 37-year-old are physically negligible so why split hairs that aren't even gray yet?) offering others no *idea* where you stand on life's continuum can cause perfectly acceptable suitors to pass you by, and that isn't going to do much for your long-term prospects as an internet flirt. Moreover, answering the age question with a rather flippant or downright sarcastic reply (Mind my own business? Ex*cuse* me?!?) makes you seem defensive and testy. And when did you last see "defensive" and "testy" come up on a list of the traits singles are looking for in Mr./Ms. Right?

Am I suggesting that you offer more information than you might have thought necessary? Perhaps I am—but with very good reason. Whether the profile service you participate in is maintained by an internet service provider or by a privately run organization, profiles are collected so that they can be used as a searchable database. That means that every salient detail you provide—from your age to the state you live in to your hobbies to your hair color—can be searched and referenced by any member who finds that particular characteristic attractive. It is easy to see how these databases benefit business. I know that my "single" designation and my self-confessed love of travel has filled my on-line mailbox with notices from electronic travel agencies. It is also easy to see how you might use a profile database as your own personal matchmaking service. If you prefer to meet men between the ages of 45 and 55 who are spiritually aware and do needlepoint for relaxation (Is Roosevelt Grier available?), all you need to do is search those options and e-mail any interesting discoveries. Conversely, anyone who is interested in scintillating conversation with a skilled flirt can presumably search and find you if you have padded your profile with the kind of details that increase your chances of being discovered.

What kind of detail works best? This is what I have found. Internet flirts are remarkably provincial. They simply can't resist searching every directory available to them for references to their home town, their favorite town, the town in which they lived as children, the college town they toilet-papered as young adults, and so on. I suggest that you include as many geographical references as make you comfortable.

For internet flirts, five years is simply too long to wait between school reunions. They invest hours searching for alumni of the colleges, universities and private schools they have attended. If you want to go to the head of your flirting class, I suggest that you include your educational affiliations in your profile.

And by all means, list your hobbies and interests, no matter how unique or even obscure you feel they may be! There may not be another eligible single in your county who is interested in the cultivation of antique roses or mud wrestling or curling (I mean the sport, not the hairstyle). But the web universe is vast and varied and I have been shocked at the diverse and far-flung people compatible profiles have brought together. Here's a case in point: My co-author, who took accordion lessons as a girl, referred rather offhandedly to the instrument in her profile. She has since heard from several people who searched the word accordion and found her, including one young man who is a member of an all-accordion rock band! Although the relationship never reached a crescendo (Barbara is happily married), their meeting was a harmonious one and they remain in contact to this day.

WHEN YOU'RE NOT YOURSELF ON THE WEB

In Japan, countless men and women cruise the 'net in the guise of the opposite gender. (It is reported that this practice is more common among young women who find adopting a male persona to be culturally and emotionally "freeing.") Here in the U.S., thousands of men and women roam cyberspace anonymously, armed with totally contrived names and profiles that are either purely fictitious or nonexistent.

There are some sound reasons for creating an alter ego whose profile and modus operandi would differ completely from your own. If you are researching the prospects for a new job, for example, or the diagnosis and treatment of an illness you may have, or any other personal subject whose discovery would subject you to embarrassment or harassment, I would certainly suggest that you do your research incognito. Likewise if you are interested in pursuing a specific fantasy or cyberspace sexual adventure. (One internet pen pal of mine who is a well-known businesswoman by day and an on-line dominatrix by night refers to her second-self as her "evil twin.") In fact, an alter ego is handy when exploring any parts of the internet where you don't necessarily want to be recognized—for whatever reason—even as a screen name. One man I know has developed an identity he uses strictly when playing the interactive trivia games offered by his internet server. He simply doesn't want to be thought of as "silly," though I have found these games to be a great way to meet new people, and that's anything but silly.

Some men and women claim that "becoming" a manufactured personality enhances their ability to interact with others, freeing them to say things they might not otherwise say, and come-on more gregariously than they might in real life. Personally, I feel interacting with others through a false identity cheats both you and those men and women with whom you flirt. A real relationship—even a real *platonic* relationship—can only be forged by two real people. And that goes double for the relationships that are conceived on the internet.

Internet acquaintances can't accept each other on "face value." The medium requires that they relate "sight-unseen." Since internet flirts must operate without gestures, looks and other visuals to judge a new friend's sincerity by, they tend to develop a modicum of healthy skepticism and a hyper-awareness of potential charlatans. Offer an answer that is not in keeping with your faux profile—and believe me, in time you will!—and you'll arouse suspicion. Reveal yourself as a fraud in an effort to put the relationship on more solid ground ("I'm not really an accountant, and I don't really water-ski barefooted but I swear, everything else I've told you is true!)" and you might as well save your breath. Your credibility has hit rock bottom. And if you reduce your chances of being snagged in a lie by offering no profile at all? Many female flirts I know won't even acknowledge e-mail from a man who will not post a profile. And I won't either. You may find yourself with plenty of time to correspond and no one to correspond with.

If you are considering adopting an alter ego so you can better impress the opposite sex, first consider what you are really looking for on the World Wide Web. If your goal is to find someone with whom you can share a good time but not necessarily a long time, then go for it! Be all you can be! It won't be long before you are found out. But if you are looking for the kind of affection and mutual respect that will endure long after your current computer is obsolete, be the charming, positive, forthright and, yes, even *flawed* person you really are. Mr. or Ms. Wrong (whom you can always identify by his or her lack of judgment) might not appreciate your candor, but the right man or woman for you most assuredly will.

ESTABLISHING YOUR IDENTITY AS A FLIRT

"Just be yourself." This good advice seems almost generic but it's hard to come off as a living, breathing dimensional being—particularly on a computer screen. I hope these tips will make it easier.

• Accentuate the positive. You might live up to the name Man-Hatr or GloomNDoom, but is that moniker likely to attract an admiring crowd? Choose a name that describes the kind of person you *want* to be and you'll become an on-screen personality that others want to be with.

• That ten-digit number may mean something to you (your high school gym locker combination? How scintillating!) but it will be utterly meaningless to anyone else. Give yourself a name, not a model number.

- Illness or misfortune is part of everyone's life so keep it in perspective. Don't allow it to engulf your on-screen identity.

- A limited profile (or no profile at all!) may result in limited prospects. Oh, it can be fun to act the Invisible Man or Woman, sneaking from chat room to game site, leaving no trace of your true identity. But providing no profile, offering no hint of your age, background or even gender, can signal that you've got something to hide (like a spouse and three kids!). More forthright men and women may choose not to chat or exchange e-mail with you until you become a little less mysterious and a little more human.

- Remember: Depth is in the details. If you are mad for Volkswagen Beetles, have taught yourself to play Mozart on a harmonica, write a little, act a little, travel or dream about traveling, don't cover your quirks as if they were an odd assortment of chocolates—put them in your profile and pass them around! The idiosyncratic jumble of skills, interests and eccentricities you've accumulated set you apart from the more mundane flirts and make you a real person in a virtual world.

5
How to Be More than a Virtual Potted Plant in a Chat Room

My friend Dana and I were exploring the chat rooms available through my internet server. Full of optimism and armed with plenty of fascinating things to say, we bopped into an over-30 singles chat area and joined the roster of internet flirts currently in the room. We were reading the chat log (the transcript of the various chats taking place simultaneously in the room) when Dana's screen name flashed onto the monitor.

"That's a hello," I notified her. "Someone is saying hello to you. Aren't you going to respond?"

Dana just shook her head.

"Why ever not?" I prompted, never one to let a willing conversational partner get away.

Dana didn't so much answer me as explode. "Because there are so many conversations going on at the same time, I can't figure out exactly what I am supposed to respond to! Am I supposed to comment on *this* conversation?" She drew her finger along the screen under a brief exchange about a singles hiking club. "Am I supposed to put my two cents' worth in on this subject?" She pointed to an ongoing debate on the merits of various Oscar nominees. "And what in the world could I possibly add to *this* conversation?" Dana indicated an ongoing argument that seemed to concern two women, one man and a face-to-face encounter that included the man and only one of the women, much to the chagrin of the other. Then she switched the machine off and smiled at me.

"I am a pretty adventurous person, but you know, Susan, this chat room thing may not be for me," Dana explained. "There are simply too many conversations going on at once. And that doesn't make me want to say hello. It makes me want to scream, 'Hey, everybody—shut up!' "

If you, like Dana, are a polite flirt who waits patiently for a lull in the conversational flow before attempting to fit a word or two in edgewise, you may be in for a long wait in the public chat room! While the one-speaker/one-topic-at-a-time rule still regulates the conversational flow in real life (depending upon the type of conversational partners you choose and their tendency to fight the current), in most chat rooms it's what I call "kamikaze conversation" that reigns supreme, where everyone says his or her piece whenever he or she chooses to say it, leaving the lurkers (and occasionally chat room hosts) to sort it out. And that's not the only drawback of electronic gab. Those of us who rely on body language to send nonverbal messages to others and to interpret the feelings of the new friends we meet are at a great loss. The subtle glances and gestures upon which we rely to make an impression (or a point) are totally out of our reach, and the only messages available for our interpretation look something like this:

CHATZALOT: So I told her, it's my way or the highway. I guess she chose the highway because
JUSTAFACTS: Age, sex, state check, pls
CHERIAMOR: 27, f, FL
WOWZAGAL: 33, f, MO
CHATZALOT: I haven't heard from her since (:-<
STEAMINMEEMY: Any women in here, 17–22?
MIKEY'SLIFE: 31, m, NYC

CHEERIO 1207: So she's gone. Now what, Chatza?
FLAKEYJANE: Hi Steamin. 23, f. Close enough?
MIKEY'SLIFE: Where in FL, Cheri?
STEAMINMEEMY: Could be close enough. Have a photo?
CHATZALOT: Now I'm looking. You don't happen to be f,
   between 33–38, do you :-,?

Disjointed? Fragmented? You bet! There are days when the chat room log reads like a Gertrude Stein poem made up entirely of the mundane, meaningless words human beings exchange upon meeting. ("An age/sex check is an age/sex check is an age/sex check . . .") Moreover, because chatters seem to have thrown off the "my turn–your turn" conversational model, the resulting free-for-all atmosphere can make each distinct conversational thread difficult to follow. Still, I have made some great friends and wonderful connections in public chat rooms, once I began to visit those chats where people who might like me (that is, people *most* like me) tend to congregate.

THE RIGHT PLACE AT THE RIGHT TIME

As a man of a "certain age," my friend Peter is particularly proud of the extent to which he has mastered his personal computer. He has even developed a tendency to show off his machine and its capabilities much the same way a new parent might display a bright, beautiful child. But one day while demonstrating the ease of on-line flirting to his neighbor, David, Peter was taught a lesson about chat room selection he won't soon forget.

All Peter intended to show David was the way chat rooms worked, so rather than search for a particular room he simply clicked into the first forum he saw: a room called "twenty-something Chat." The conversation was lively but alien to Peter and David. Consequently, they didn't participate at all until one chatter suggested an age/sex check. Laughing at the disparity between their ages and the median age of the other participants, Peter typed in his true age, expecting to be ignored. He was not.

"Yikes! A grown-up!" shrieked one chatter.

"You don't belong in this room!" bellowed another.

Not one to be daunted by issues like age, Peter remained cheerful and open. "In what room do I belong?" he asked.

"The over-forty room," suggested one chatter.

"The funeral home," suggested another.

Peter reported this gaff to me with some embarrassment. The twenty-somethings had made him feel like a "leering codger." Weren't they guilty of ageism? Weren't they closed-minded, inconsiderate flirts? My answer was a resounding yes . . . and no.

In my years of experience as an internet flirt, I have never found it necessary to insult anyone I have met on the web. On the whole, I have found that people who annoy me are easily ignored—or, in extreme cases, turned in on a terms-of-service violation. So the twenty-somethings showed their immaturity when they turned their curiosity about Peter's presence in the room into a personal attack.

On the other hand, they had reason for a modicum of healthy suspicion. After all, what was Peter, a man of fifty-plus, doing in the room? Was he a computerized Humbert Humbert? A sexual predator? A parent? A spy? I explained to Peter that although the room was designated for use by "twenty-somethings," many of the chatters would be several years younger than that. A 17-to-20-year-old who had been warned about deceptive, sophisticated, mature strangers like him would almost certainly view Peter as a threat. They simply would not feel comfortable resuming their conversation unless they abandoned the room themselves or drove Peter from it.

"Oh! Then what are you suggesting? That I avoid that particular chat room?" Peter gave me a good-natured elbow in the ribs. "I thought you told me that a good internet flirt should visit every possible kind of chat room?"

I admit to you, as I admitted to Peter, that that is my advice, all right. The fact is, since I have been chat-browsing, I have learned a little more about a great many things, from what the latest research on pheromones reveals (hold on to your wallet), to the hottest singles vacation spots in the Caribbean, to the benefits of feng shui upon the late-model automobile interior (don't ask). Has this knowledge made me a better person? Probably not, but it has certainly made me a more adept flirt! All the most successful flirts know a little something about everything, and can speak charmingly and intelligently on virtually any subject that matters to his conversational partner. To me, visiting far-flung chats is the technological age equivalent of finishing school. It broadens your horizons and adds poise, depth and an air of mystery to your communication. Moreover, as far as I am concerned, exploring any and all of the chat rooms fit for human habitation (and perhaps a few that aren't) is a pastime virtually without pitfalls. Rejection is never face to face, so being ignored or insulted lacks its usual sting. You can abandon a dull or incompatible chat site for a new locale in a matter of seconds. You can scan the profiles for the next Mr. or Ms. Right while wearing your broken-in bathrobe. And considering the virtually endless supply of chats ranging in quality and type from the good, to the bad, to the downright ugly, you can meet thousands of men and women without ever entering a room where you will be directed to the nearest undertaker or mistaken for a sexual predator.

Of course, flitting from site to site is really no substitute for finding a handful of chats that feel just right for you. A comfortable chat room should make you feel welcome on arrival, encourage your participation while you're there and entice you to visit again, like a favorite real-life hangout. It should attract a tolerant and easygoing crowd, be free of secret agendas and allow you to be your most sparkling self. How do you know when you've found such a forum? I've identified three factors that always pinpoint the right chat:

- A great room is based upon your hobbies and interests. A chat that focuses upon your favorite pastime or avocation gives you an instant in with like-minded people. Use it! At the very least, you'll pick up a few pointers on seascape painting, snowboarding or ghost hunting, and you may pick up a new companion to share your hobby with.

- A compatible site allows you to fix your sights on your long-term romantic goal. Many "flirting" rooms are about cybersex, not relating. If what you're looking for is a good time, go for it. But if you're interested in finding a relationship that will last a long time, look elsewhere. Internet romance only works when you find a partner who gets to know *you*—not your sexual predilections.

• An open, accepting chat room encourages you to express your personality. I have been in chats where a simple greeting seems to fall on deaf ears. I have also been in chats where even the most innocuous comment is met with criticism, hostility or total banishment. There is no reason to subject yourself to the whims of an insular group of defensive, inbred chatters.

You will know the best chat for you because you will feel that you "know" the guileless and approachable men and women who meet there. You will recognize them as people who understand what you are saying, and they will assume that you will understand them, as well. That feeling of "simpatico" is difficult to define, but you can always tell it by the liberating effect it has on conversation—and flirting.

Of course, I am not recommending that you sign in to any particular chat room and settle in for the long haul. That would be like spending every evening in the same club where you are exposed nightly to the same group of people and choose your companions from the same dating pool. The internet is a much larger neighborhood than the one you currently inhabit. It's time you got to know the exciting men and women who make that virtual neighborhood such an exhilarating place.

SIX SENSATIONAL CONVERSATION STIMULATORS

"Great," commented Jane, a marketing student who attended one of my flirting seminars. "Now I feel like I have a zillion chat rooms to visit and no idea what to say when I get there!"

To be honest, arriving at a site without a script—or even a broken-in, comfortable line—isn't such a bad thing. There is a tremendous amount an observant flirt can learn while just lurking (listening in but not participating) in an unfamiliar chatatorium. Is this a public chat room that has been taken over by a group of regulars? Tune in for a few minutes and you'll find out whether newbies are truly welcome or not. Is this chat a little too staid, racy, technical or just plain dull for you? You'll know before long whether to join in or log off. Are these chatters the kind of people you'd choose to be around in a real-world setting? If not, relief is just a click away. And you'll know what sorts of sites to avoid in the future.

Still, it is simply self-defeating to find yourself tongue-tied when you're visiting a chat room. Since your fellow chatters cannot become intrigued by your physical charms, there is no incentive for them to attempt to draw you out. Besides, maintaining one's silence in a chat room is like hiding a vast fortune in your mattress. You might minimize your risk of losing your emotional investment, but what are you likely to gain?

For every flirt obsessing about what to say and how to say it, there are ten eligible singles wishing that some attractive stranger would say something—*anything*—just to break the ice. The conversation starters may seem a tad coquettish, somewhat obvious or even a bit contrived, but they have worked for me in a wide variety of rooms from "Manhattan Melee" (geographically based chats always provide plenty of fertile conversational terrain) to "Car Talk" (where the helpful, knowledgeable motorheads are). Find one or two that do the trick for you and you are on your way to expanding your address book and your horizons.

1. *"What an insightful/funny/interesting comment. Are you a psychologist/comic/expert?"* Everyone loves a compliment. Nevertheless, positive reinforcement is rarely offered in the chats I have visited. And compliments that flatter while encouraging the happy recipient to reveal something more about his or her personal life are harder to come by than a postage stamp in Bill Gates' mailbag. Since everyone responds to validation, why not give that particularly charming chatter the affirmation he or she deserves? It's the least you can do for someone who's attracted you and held your attention. Just be sure to keep your compliments sincere and use them in moderation. Even the most casual comments can take on weight when they appear in print in the full view of others.

2. *"You know so much about (insert subject). Can you recom-*

mend a good (insert your shared special interest here) site?" Believe me, this question can get you a lot further than the next interesting website! People *love* to talk about their interests and hobbies, and they can't resist sharing what they've learned with any eager apprentice who is just beginning to explore an area of interest. So, whether your conversational partner has expressed an interest in 1960s pop art, organic gardening, reggae music or Monty Python trivia, it would certainly behoove you to ask him or her to point you toward a particularly informative related website. The least that will happen is that you will learn something about a new topic or field of interest. What will most likely happen is that your conversational partner will ask you to e-mail him or her with your thoughts after you visit the site. And that's all it takes to launch a very simpatico on-line friendship.

3. *"What would surprise me most about you?"* and other open-ended questions (questions that can't be answered with a simple yes or no) never fail to break the ice. That's because they encourage respondents to expound on what is almost certainly a favorite subject: themselves. And since they offer a non-threatening alternative to the ubiquitous age/sex/location check, open-ended questions also tend to attract a wittier, more thoughtful and emotionally informed respondent—one who would certainly make for an interesting on-line romance.

Be aware, however, that some open-ended questions can be considered extremely personal, and therefore threatening. So keep the interrogatory light (no questions about sex, religion, politics, past relationships or other hot topics, please) and be prepared to share your own answer to the question you have asked. If it is uncomfortable for you to reveal, it will certainly unnerve your conversational partner. Putting a new friend on the hot seat is never good flirting.

4. *"I'll bet there's a story behind that quotation!"* Nearly every internet user's profile includes a personal quotation, and nearly every quotation chosen represents a life lesson or story that is meaningful to your on-line pal. Commenting on an especially funny, wise or provocative quote sends the message that you were interested enough in your chat room acquaintance to search his or her profile without making you appear overly eager. (Everyone

checks out others' profiles, right?) Most of all, encouraging him or her to reveal the quote's significance opens the lines of communication and deepens and extends the conversation. You'll get to know something about each other—how you think, what you value, which values you share—that will give you a strong foundation for an ongoing friendship.

5. *Repeat. Rephrase. Reflect.* Those of you who read my first book, *How to Attract Anyone, Anytime, Anyplace,* or who have attended my seminars will recognize this "active listening" technique as the key to helping a new friend to open up, making him or her feel validated and secure in your company and turning a casual acquaintance into a close confrere. And the best news is this simple strategy is effective whether you are "working" a real-life room full of singles or your favorite chat. All you need to do is subtly repeat and rephrase any statement that catches your interest ("You say you spend an average of 15 hours a day on the internet? Isn't that something!") and keep reflecting the focus of the conversation back to your conversational partner. ("You may be the consummate internet flirt! Have you met many promising prospects?") I guarantee it won't be long—perhaps only two or three minutes—before your conversational partner has revealed enough about him- or herself to convince you that he or she is ripe for further discourse or that you simply need to find a chat room further away from this person.

6. *"Oh, you're from (city/state/country)! Is my favorite museum/restaurant/hotspot still at the corner of (exact location)?"* Most of the time, age/sex/location information just breezes past most chat participants. They've become numb to it, much the same way they cease to see the pesky ads that punctuate certain screens. But why not stir up a little commonality by turning what you learn about a new friend's life stage and location into a conversation starter?

Most people have carefully chosen the city/state they call home. In most cases it is safe to assume they will be partial to the place they live. By offering a positive comment about their general location you send a message that you appreciate their taste and feel "at home" in their environs, and that's the sort of commonality that can really help a flirt to get one foot in the door. And if you have actually spent time in a chat room friend's city or state, so much the better! Being able to cite specific landmarks and favorite haunts provides you with instant conversational fodder. Moreover, it communicates the possibility that you may visit your acquaintance's home city or state again, which never fails to enhance your geographical desirability, whether you truly intend to visit that particular region again or not.

You will note that many topics and techniques that pass as conversation starters in the chat room you frequent—some, perhaps, that you yourself have used—are not listed here. That's because although these subjects and strategies are common in chats, I have found them to be nearly always conversational dead ends. These conversation killers include pouring out your soul about a current problem (makes you appear needy and frightening), offering advice (solicited or not, right or wrong, advising someone you don't know on a problem you are ignorant of is a no-win situation), criticizing the opinions of others (Who died and made you the final arbiter of good taste, high standards and common sense? Nobody. So get over it.), interrupting the conversational flow (no matter how inane it may be) and, of course, sexual innuendo. ('Net users, particularly female 'net users, can be extremely sensitive about potential sexual predators. Is your prurient comment or risqué joke so important that you would risk casting yourself in anything but the most flattering light?)

Practice makes the perfect flirt—and chat rooms offer a virtually endless supply of eligible men and women with whom you can perfect your communication skills. Just maintain an upbeat, attentive and open attitude and you'll find yourself in great demand. And if you still have trouble finding the right conversational partners, try the technique below.

STRUCTURED MINGLING

"Oh, I've met many men on the internet who were just right," said Marlee with a wry grin. "There was Nathan; he was just right for my sister, Karen. And there was Chip; he turned out to be just right for my neighbor Dan. Too bad what I can't seem to find is a 'net friend who is just right for *me*!"

If I have said it once, I have said it a thousand times: Flirting is a numbers game. Your mission as a master-flirt-in-training is to enhance your odds of finding that one-in-a-million match by meeting as many potential prospects as you can, exploring commonality when you find it and quickly moving on when you do not. The single men and women who have taken my seminars have reported to me that by "working the room" in this way, they have been able to meet most of the eligible singles in any face-to-face setting, pass their cards or telephone numbers to the lucky few they found most interesting, then move on to the next party and a whole new group of prospects all in the space of a single evening. I am pleased to announce that this foolproof approach, which I call "structured mingling," can also be used in a chat room where the total number of potential partners is not limited by fire department regulations, and a new group of fascinating, dynamic singles is only a click (rather than a cab ride) away.

Chat rooms are notoriously distracting places. Spend ten minutes with a talkative group of book lovers in a room called "La Bibliothèque" and you will almost certainly forget you're there to find a partner, not a page-turner. The goal of structured mingling, then, is to minimize such distractions by focusing on meeting as many compatible men or women as possible, establishing commonality, then moving on—after adding each newfound romantic interest to your address book—to the next compatible conversational partner.

I structure my "mingling" sessions this way: First, I carefully select a chat room where the subject is a hobby or special interest of mine or which culls its participants from a demographic group I find appealing. That way, the chat room does my prescreening for me. Then, after a brief "lurk around" to get my bearings, I introduce myself to a chatter who seems compatible, set the timer on my computer for three minutes then chat away! If in the allotted time I find that my new friend and I have nothing in common, I thank him for what has been a pleasant interlude and seek alternative companionship. If, on the other hand, I discover that we share an interest, hobby or attitude or if we simply "hit it off," I enjoy his company until the timer goes off then ask him if I can add his name to my little black book and move on to the next conversational partner.

Oh, I can just hear you now: "It takes me months to find a man or woman I like and you are telling me not to spend more than three minutes chatting with him or her?" Yes, I am—unless you are a very poor typist, in which case I will allow you five. In my years as an on-line flirt, I have found that three minutes is more than enough time to make a positive impression, establish commonality and leave 'em clamoring for more. But perhaps more to the point, three minutes is not long enough to become dull or repetitive, to find yourself in the middle of some pointless chat room argument or harrangue, or to enter into a cybersex liaison which may give your ego a temporary boost but, I repeat, has nothing to do with good flirting. Besides, knowing that the clock is ticking reminds me that I must project my wittiest, most charming self, and *very* expeditiously. In a very real sense, setting a time limit goads me into making the best impression possible. Since the timer has become such an important tool for me, I don't leave my homepage without it.

Do I expect you to always limit yourself to three-minute chats? Certainly not! The structured chat is an exercise, and an exciting diversion. It's purpose is to remind you of just how many eligible men and women are available to you on the 'net and how simple it can be to meet them if you keep an open mind. Remember: Every relationship you've ever envied began with a simple hello. Why not invest half an hour in saying as many hellos as possible? Do it once and you've made contact with ten exciting new partners. Do it once a week and the possibilities are endless.

Besides, just because you've only invested three minutes in the relationship doesn't mean the relationship will only last three minutes! There will be plenty of good times and shared experiences to come, if you take care to end the chat but not the relationship. And that means . . .

CLOSING THE DEAL

"I met the most amazing man in the musician's chat!" my friend Risa, an accomplished saxophonist, gushed. "First we discussed the difficulties of making the transition between keyboard and brass instruments. Then we exchanged pictures. After we discovered that we had attended the same awful music camp as kids, we ended up chatting for four hours . . . until three-thirty in the morning!"

"So what now?" I prompted.

"I don't know." Risa shrugged. "I haven't heard from him since."

Are dynamic, fascinating and seemingly straightforward men and women a vanishing breed? They must be. Otherwise, why do so many of our most promising prospects charm us, ask where they can reach us, vow they'll be in contact then disappear, never to be heard from again?

If you, like Risa, are trying to understand whether there really is a mysterious vortex like the Bermuda Triangle pulling in unsuspecting suitors—or whether we can arrange for one—you may be heartened to learn that there are a lot of reasons partners run hot then cold (or simply run for the hills). Many of these vanishing lotharios are secretly committed to someone else and have thought better of pursuing you. Some have been hurt in previous relationships and are gun-shy. Others are negative-thinking flirts who are so certain a new love will end badly (as did past relationships), they simply withdraw without explanation. But in my opinion, more often than not, the audacious charmers who charge our gangplanks tonight only to jump ship tomorrow do so not because they are fearful or wounded, they get away simply because we let them.

A new friendship is a fragile and frightening mix of promise and risk. No man wants to stick his neck out with a woman he has not known long enough to trust. And no woman is comfortable expressing her interest in a suitor who may not share her ardor. But unless we telegraph our feelings, we will never discover whether those feelings are reciprocal. And unless we let our internet heart-throbs know—without appearing too eager, too desperate or too "easy"—that we have found them to be special, intriguing and just as real to us as the men and women we meet face to face, they will simply disappear from our chat logs forever, and evaporate into the electronic ozone.

How does the master internet flirt end a particularly enchanting chat, structured or otherwise, without ending the friendship? Here are some ideas that work for me.

Take an instant to establish intimacy. Instant messaging— sending those private messages that pop up in the corner of the screen—is an ideal way to make an immediate and personal connection with a particularly magnetic and personable chat participant. Best of all, IM capability is now available to you regardless of which internet provider you are using.

Instant messages are a popular and effective means of establishing contact with those winning personalities who distinguish themselves as room "standouts." Simply fill out the instant message box with your correspondent's screen name, add an intriguing but non-threatening message (this is a great opportunity to compliment the chat-whiz who made you think or chuckle out loud) and hit the send button. Your message will be delivered in a nanosecond. (Note: Some systems ask the recipient whether he or she accepts your instant message before sending it through.)

A few tips. Since men tend to outnumber women on-line, women can be inundated with IMs. It is crucial that male internet flirts display their imagination, winning humor and good manners in their IMs in order to separate themselves from the rabble. I also hasten to point out that many internet flirts make it a practice to ignore any instant message that includes such tacky phraseology as "What are you wearing right now?" or "My monitor seemed to be overheating. Then I noticed you were in the chat room." or "Hey, honey—wanna cyber?" Lurid comments from cyber-jerks aren't any more attractive than lewd suggestions from any other obnoxious stranger. Keep up the smarmy chatter and you will find yourself deleted from the chat room goings-on (a chat room bully is easy to bypass: You simply highlight the offender's name and hit your ignore button) and from any possibility of future contact.

How do I use my IM feature to close the deal with a chat room friend? I use a formula that has worked for me for years, which

I call the 3-S's. First I stroke. ("Your responses have been so witty/charming/on the money.") Then I suggest. ("I'd really love to get to know you better.") And finally, I solidify a plan or meeting time. ("Could we chat another time? In this room, perhaps? Or privately?")

I think of this direct, yet non-threatening approach as the on-line equivalent of asking an attractive man or woman to meet you for coffee. It puts the ball directly into the invitee's court. He may suggest that you exchange e-mail. She may prefer that you meet in a public chat room, therefore keeping your rendezvous fairly public. The point is that you have given your conversational partner every option to remain within his or her comfort zone, and that kind of consideration paves the way for a very comfortable second meeting.

Go private. A private chat takes place in a room just big enough for two—or however many lucky prospects you choose to invite—away from the prying eyes of a public chat group. It enables you to tune in to each other without having to tune out the chaos of six or seven other ongoing conversations, and sets the stage for deeper, more intimate discourse. The problem is that, having just met, you may have precious little to say to each other, and nothing is more awkward than having little to say in an otherwise silent room.

Before you close the deal by inviting your new friend to join you in a private chat, be sure that you have already established a broad spectrum of shared interests and/or experiences (and perhaps a written list of open-ended questions) should the conversation lag.

Be a buddy! To have a friend, be a friend! And there is no better way to establish a friendship, develop intimacy and just stay in contact with a promising prospect than to add that special person to your buddy list.

The buddy list is among my favorite features offered by my internet server. I love it! Essentially a database in which you can enter the names of your friends, family members and business contacts, your buddy list appears each time you sign on to let you know if one of your "buddies" happens to be on-line. You then have the option of IMing a brief greeting, sending him or her an electronic greeting card or simply picking up your conversation where you last left off.

Be aware, however, that it is good manners to ask for a new friend's permission before adding him or her to your list. It can be off-putting to receive a barrage of IMs from someone you feel you hardly know—and downright unnerving to think that a virtual stranger is notified each time you sign on. So be sure you get the green light before proceeding, and don't buddy before you are ready.

Hey, look me over! One of the most pleasant deal-closers came to me via a very charming guy from the West Coast. Larry and I had chatted briefly, then I signed off. The next day I found a lovely e-mail from him thanking me for a pleasant conversation and inviting me to download and view his photo. I did, I was impressed by his laugh lines and I e-mailed him back. Though we are not a love-match (I am not interested in relocating and neither is he), we remain on-line buddies.

While one of the benefits of on-line flirtation is that it enables us to get past the purely physical, it can be great to have, on file and ready to send, a photograph you are comfortable forwarding to on-line acquaintances. Oh, sure, your jokes are provocative and your observations titillating, but they only exist as ideas. A photo makes you "real." And your willingness to send one communicates that you are honest, too. (How many internet flirts really look like Kim Basinger or Leonardo DiCaprio? How many claim to? Case closed.) Besides, sending a photo gives you the opportunity to show off that killer smile and display those bedroom eyes, and that never hurts, either.

Send an electronic nice-breaker. Those of you who have read my two previous books know two things about me: that I will talk to virtually anyone, anytime, anyplace, and that I pass out "nice-breakers" the way New York meter maids pass out parking tickets. What are nice-breakers? They are the convenient, business-sized cards I pass along to each gentleman I meet to let him know that I'd like to know him better. (An excellent example of a nice-breaker appears at the end of my book *101 Ways to Flirt*.)

Well, the good news is that the internet is the ideal hunting ground for a single woman who likes to chat up everyone she meets, especially if she happens to have a few electronic nice-breakers up her sleeve! The electronic nice-breaker message can be something as simple as this: *It's difficult to get to know each other meeting screen-to-screen, but I'd like to try. Please e-mail: (type address).*

If you're especially creative, you can add a nice clip-art border and save it to a handy file. When the mood to make a move strikes, just copy and e-mail. Your mailbox won't be empty for long, believe me.

ALL TALK . . . AND MAYBE SOME ACTION

Any chat room can be a great place to make friends, network, practice your flirting skills or kindle romance—so let's hear some chatter out there! Just be sure to consider these guidelines as you cruise the chats. They've transformed many singles from men and women who used to just chat about romance to the chronically overbooked, never-overlooked men and women who live it!

• Lurk awhile to get your bearings in a new chat room. You'll increase your odds if you tune in to the topic and wait to see whether this is a haven for an exclusive group of "regulars" or happy hunting ground for elegible newcomers.

• Greet the room upon your arrival, excuse yourself if you are interrupting an ongoing conversation and don't ever try to change the subject to one that is more to your liking. Be as polite in the chats as you would at a club and you'll make points as a polished, refined flirt.

• Be open to approaches by others. I know one newbie who signs off every time she receives an IM from a man she doesn't know! If you are flustered by the friendly messages that pop up on your screen, prepare yourself before ever signing-on. Rehearse a cordial greeting, script some open-ended questions. Sometimes we singles get so hung up on how and when to flirt with others we overlook those who are desperately trying to flirt with us!

• If your chats seem to meander without purpose or you feel that you're chatting with everyone but meeting no one, try a structured chat. And vow that you won't say good-bye to the fascinating cyberflirts you meet unless you . . .

• Close the deal by suggesting—and agreeing to—a future chat or internet "meeting." Don't put yourself in a position to bemoan the one that got away.

6
The Personal Touch

Attractive SWM seeks female partner/companion, age 18–35. Loves sunsets, holding hands, and long, leisurely strolls on the beach. If you want to join me for some special moments, shared pleasures and old-fashioned romance, e-mail _____.

As an experiment, I invited six of the most perceptive and fun single women I knew to join me for lunch. The crème brûlée was still quivering on our dessert plates when I served up this tempting tidbit I found on a popular internet personals site. What follows is a smorgasbord of my friends' comments.

"Oh, he's attractive, is he? To whom? His mother?"
"Seeks female companion eighteen to thirty-five? How old is this guy anyway?"
"Seeks partner/companion? Does this guy want a *girlfriend*? A *wife*? Or a Labrador retriever?"
"Oh, what do you know—he loves sunsets and walks on the beach! Who doesn't? Even Adolf Hitler liked mountain climbing, but that didn't make him a sensitive, caring person, did it?" "Join him for 'special moments'? Oh, I get it. He's one of those 'the best things in life are free' types.

Well I want 'special.' But that doesn't mean I don't want dinner, too!"

Listening to a group of "been-there, done-that" singles dissect a personal ad, particularly if it is the kind of an ad you might have written yourself, can be painful. But learning what works and what doesn't when you're playing the internet personals game is certainly worth your time, effort and maybe even a little trial and error.

Personal ads are hot and heavy on the World Wide Web. Featured in thousands of separate websites targeted specifically for the burgeoning singles market and in countless more that garner their entries from professional associations, sport and hobby aficionados, national organizations and other specialty sites where like-minded individuals gather, the on-line personals have become *the* way to meet a virtually unlimited supply of unattached men and women, communicate with any and all of the men and women you "click" with, and fill your on-line address book to the crashing point with new friends, consequential contacts and possible paramours.

So what have these electronic personals got that newspaper and magazine ads have not? Plenty! A magazine or newspaper known to be a hot spot for personals placement might have a circulation of 70,000 up to 500,000. But a booming on-line site can field more than a million hits a day, and the largest networks routinely do! Any ad you place will have a virtually unlimited audience, and that means unlimited opportunities for flirting! In addition, placing your ad electronically is more economical. Upscale magazines—particularly those known for their high-quality match-making pages—can charge up to thirty-seven dollars per line of text for ads that run only one month. Web personals are often free (though some charge an easily affordable fee or membership to site) and can run as long as three months to several years before being renewed. Plus, internet sites make it easy for an interested party to respond to an ad. There's no stationery to choose (Are flowers too feminine? Is letterhead too professional?), no stamps to buy and no hassles if you choose the right site in which to display your ad.

SETTING YOUR SITES

All sites are not created equal where personals are concerned, and the level of success you experience depends on choosing one that is equal to the task of attracting quality responses.

Just to get an idea of the range of sites available to you, I suggest that you key words like "singles, matchmaking" and "relationships" into your search engine. This will reap you so many links to explore, it will fill your nights and days and leave you no time for flirting! I suggest that you visit ten, including large and small sites, just to get your feet wet, then consider your options.

There are two general types of personals spaces: large, singles-oriented, well-visited sites whose purpose is general matchmaking (men in search of women, men in search of men, women in search of women, etc.) and smaller, more narrowly targeted, interest-oriented sites whose goal is matchmaking within a specific group of people (i.e. single parents, Jewish or Christian singles, antique collectors, readers of certain magazines, etc.). Each of these types of sites serves a specific clientele, from the "more-the-merrier" flirts who simply don't feel as though they're "out there" unless their mailboxes are bursting with e-mail, to those more discerning men and women who prefer to hear only from a select group of respondents.

You will also find that personals sites differ significantly when it comes to ease of use. Some make navigation easy and fun, providing simple, step-by-step directions for placing an ad, as well as easy-to-use point and click features for searching the personals in their databanks. Since both directly affect your ability to find compatible pen friends and make it either a snap or a snafu for others to find *you*, I suggest that you set aside some time to explore and see which sites might route the most traffic in your direction. I, for instance, like to arrange to meet my internet friends when I travel (or have someone right around the corner when I don't!). I also have some specific requirements in a man. Therefore, it is important to me that ads are easily searched geographically and by category.

It is also important to me that I receive the most possible responses to each personal ad I place, and that those responses are tailored to suit my particular desires and needs. I know that, on the surface, that statement seems like a contradiction, but really it is not. I have always been a woman who preferred to cast a wide net (there are a lot of fish in the sea, after all) but not so wide and deep that I am hauling up seaweed and muck along with the catch of the day. As a result, I prefer to do my fishing in many ponds and place several ads at a time—one at a large site and perhaps two or three more at more exclusive locales. I also write my ads very carefully to gently discourage those swains whose needs and hankerings conflict with my own. (I do not solicit responses from men who are in a less settled stage of life, who do not like to travel or still want children. That would simply waste my time and theirs.)

On the whole, the on-line personals are a very safe, rewarding and fun venue for establishing contact with a virtually limitless number of possible friends and lovers. Whether you are posting an ad or responding to one, the personals afford you a great many benefits over the chat room milieu. For instance, the interaction doesn't take place in front of an audience. Others judge you on the basis of an in-depth, thoughtfully composed ad, not a ten-line profile you wrote in the first five minutes after signing-on with your server. You can take all the time you need to decide whether to respond to a friendly overture. You are in total control of the rate at which any relationship develops—or whether it develops at all. The personals don't usually generate flames or other unpleasant e-mail. And because there is always the possibility you may actually want to meet a pen friend face to face, it isn't as tempting for personals users to assume fanciful (or fraudulent) personalities.

The down side to the personals? As some of my more writer's-cramped friends will tell you, the only pitfall is that you must write an ad—or respond to one—to participate. And that task can be unnerving to the poetically challenged.

I hope these tips will make the process easier.

WRITING YOUR AD

Vivid, exciting writing begins in the same hot spot that inspires great sex: the brain. Therefore, you must begin the writing process by carefully considering what kind of person you truly are and the type of man or woman you want to respond to your ad.

I know what you're thinking. Who has time to make a list of all my dazzling characteristics? I suggest that you make time. Too many otherwise wonderful men and women dwell on their short-comings and are not cognizant enough of the many attributes that make them special to others. Putting the qualities that make you unique into writing will make them real to you. Consequently, your personal ad will not read like a puff piece, but a real representation of the traits you have to offer.

And if making a list brings a hint of reality to the way you think of and present yourself, it will also bring your search for a significant other down to earth. Personals sites can be dauntingly large. You may feel that you are being overwhelmed with too many choices. Listing the qualities that truly please you in a lover, partner or friend will help you to separate the promising prospects whose traits, interests and habits you deeply value, from the intriguing but probably not-long-term-material men and women you might not want to hear from.

When your lists are complete and you have considered your options, it is time to write your "headline" or "grabber." A head-line sets the tone of your ad. A creative and compelling headline will also "grab" the attention of the kind of men and women you are hoping to attract, so it is very important. There are three basic types of headlines currently in use—straightforward:

SWM hiker, 28, ISO adventurous SW

clever:

Baritone, 36, seeks lady who'll make his heart sing

and a particularly vivid type I call "representative":

Leo DiCaprio type seeks SW, 18–25 who won't abandon ship

While there is nothing wrong with using a straightforward headline (they are the mainstay of singles who don't want to come off as too cutesy), bear in mind that such to-the-point, no-nonsense dispatches are a dime a dozen at the larger personals sites. Consequently, your ad may not attract as many responses as it should. If you are a naturally funny flirt or if you have a way with words, you might try a clever lead. A robust sense of humor ranks high on the list of what most favored men and women are looking for in an internet acquaintance and personality is always a favored trait in "what you want in mate/date" quizzes. But if you will only settle for the sort of headline you find most attractive in others' personals and have reaped the greatest return that way, opt for the representative headline.

When we meet and are attracted by others in the real world, events progress as follows: First, we note our partner's physical appeal. If he or she makes a positive physical impression, we initiate a conversation. When we interact on the internet, however, physicality—on which we usually base our first impressions—is missing. By supplying the singles who will read your personal ad with a concrete image that expresses your personality and preferences, you restore the physical aspect of the attraction process. You also create a vivid, "nearly real" first impression in the mind of everyone who browses your ad. Since many people have a better memory for faces than they do for names, descriptions and other abstract information, painting a mental picture of yourself will speak louder than words and leave a more lasting memory. They'll remember that outdoorsy Picabo Street type or distinguished Walter Cronkite clone when it comes time to separate the possibilities from the also-rans.

Beyond composing the perfect headline, you must present the facts, and just the facts—a task some singles tell me can be rather daunting. The good news is that it is nearly impossible to leave critically important information out of your ad. Virtually every personals site suggests that you fill out a personal information form, thus ensuring that their subscribers will have easy access to such basics as your age range (more on that later), your occupation, religion, race, smoking/drinking status, a general physical description and a brief description of the type of companion you are looking for.

I would also suggest that you provide certain other pieces of information near the beginning of your listing, even if these biographical tidbits are not specifically requested. These include your sexual preferences, geographical range and any behavior, habit or affiliation that is a definite turn-off for you, like religion or race. I love browsing the personals. But if I had a quarter for every ad I have read (and some of these ads are longer than my divorce decree!) only to discover somewhere on the bottom of page four that the writer, who seemed like my soul mate, simply won't settle for anything but a Houston-based, Protestant brunette who shares his penchant for naked polo, I'd be a millionaire several times over. So if there are some specific requirements you are looking to fulfill, put them up front where people can see it.

I also advise you to be specific, but keep it brief. I have seen other "experts" advise ad-writers to keep to a three-to-five computer screen maximum. I am telling you to submit no more than three paragraphs—*total*. This guideline provides you with plenty of room to express your sparkling personality, detail your preferences and even include a little wit. What it does not allow you is the opportunity to spin such a lengthy yarn you will ultimately hang yourself. Bear in mind that your goal is to dazzle your audience, then leave them wanting more. Immerse them in the blow-by-blow history of your failed marriage, your fascinating (but only to you) against-all-odds climb to success or your life-transforming near-death experience and you are almost certainly telling more than anyone wants to know.

What else doesn't the reader want to know? In brief, your medical history, your pet peeves, the disappointments of your lifetime, and any hopes you may have for those men or women who respond to your ad that involve nudity. Even if sex is on your mind, keep it out of your copy. Your ad is, after all, an introduction. Add sex to the text and you also introduce the possibility that you are either too socially inept to attract sexual partners or dangerously sexually obsessed.

If you are unsure that your ad paints an accurate and interesting portrait of you, or if you are uncertain of your writing skills, ask a more literary friend to take a look at your work before you post it. Good writers use words to make an impression that is as interesting and complex as they are. Less skilled wordsmiths tend to post descriptions that seem pale in comparison to the real thing. The ability to create compelling, intimate, descriptive writing is a rare trait. Ask a more experienced flirt to critique your ad and edit out any obvious errors. In the personals game, as in real life, what goes around comes around. An ad that is rife with misused words, misspellings and grammatical errors is unlikely to elicit a response from any well-educated man or woman.

Last but certainly not least, *be sincere*. Smart singles have a healthy cynicism about personal ads in general and internet personals in particular. How could it be otherwise? Either the internet is the only place where every woman looks like Sandra Bullock and every man reminds people of John F. Kennedy, Jr. or there are more than a few truth stretchers on-line.

Just as in chat rooms, there is no reason to air your most intimate laundry in a personal ad or spill your guts about every detail of your life, but lying is another matter entirely. Making others believe you are someone or something you aren't defeats your purpose as a flirt. It skews communication at every level and makes a meaningful connection impossible.

Then again, there are issues where complete candor may work against you, as my friend Georgia was quick to point out. Georgia's last husband was twelve years younger than she. The boyfriend she met soon after the divorce was nearly five years younger than her husband.

"I love younger men, and younger men love me. But do you think I would attract the kind of man I'm looking for if the first line of my personal ad contained the number forty-eight? I don't think so," Georgia told me. "So don't wait for me to reveal my age in a personal ad . . . not until Disney rewrites *Snow White* so that the prince rides off with the old queen rather than the dewy-skinned princess."

Georgia has a point. Age can be a sore subject especially to the beautiful, mature women who must fight the cultural effects of ageism, though men are certainly not immune. When composing a personal ad, it is tempting to simply pass over the subjects that can prejudice others against us, including age, weight, race, religion, etc. My advice to Georgia, and to anyone else who refuses to allow stereotyping to limit their social options, is to paint the issue in the best light, *but don't lie*. For instance, Georgia isn't forty-eight, she's a "child of the sixties." My neighbor, Jordan, who has dated women from 19 to 35, isn't 27—he's "an adventurous Aquarian." By the way, I have never gotten more responses in my life than I did when, by mistake, my age was listed in a personal ad as 98! I'd mixed up the current year with my age. You would think that the gaffe would have meant the end of any responses for me—other than from EMS—but the funny, utterly charming responses are pouring in, and have included a master flirt who complimented me on how great I looked for my age, and a humorous guy who asked if 102 was too old for me.

If you still can't settle on an adjective or two that represents your age/weight/type without being as explicit as, say, a birth certificate or passport, you might try one or more of the subjective alternatives below:

32 Ways to Say "I'm Attractive!"

What's in a word? More than you may suspect! Of course, every word has a specific definition, but it also carries a nuance or connotation that sends a message all its own. Here is a selection of descriptive words that will make your ad more appealing to others without giving them too much information:

energetic	caring	romantic	upbeat
positive	adventurous	healthy	exciting
warm	open	dependable	discriminating
busy	creative	true	secure
fun-loving	dynamic	bright	independent
high-spirited	witty	sensitive	mellow
vibrant	polished	accomplished	dashing
professional	sporty	articulate	outgoing

32 Words that Send the Message "I'm Iffy"

young at heart	zealous	nonconformist	nonmaterialistic
voluptuous	provocative	competitive	one of a kind
crazy	leisure-lover	excitable	loner

"Good time	single-minded	wild	not obsessed
Charlie"	interesting	old-fashioned	with looks
"Merry	unique	sensible	earthy
widow"	quiet	ample	party animal
meticulous	eccentric	domestic	complex
opinionated	husky/burly	demure	beer can
intense			collector

CONFRONTING THE "P" WORD

"I'm ready to place my personal ad," announced Cindy, a college student who attended one of my seminars. "But where can I have a photo taken?"

Believing she was referring to a digital photo which is easily imported to a computer location, I began to run down the list of print-to-disk conversion houses in the neighborhood. But Cindy stopped me.

"No, no—that's not what I mean," she corrected. "What I mean is, where can I have a photo taken that will make me look like Cindy Crawford?"

If the idea of publishing a photo along with your personal ad compels you to search not for an available scanner but for an alternate face—and believe me, many swell-looking male and female flirts are extremely photo-phobic—then my advice to you is, why bother? A photo is not necessary. In many cases, it is not even recommended.

The simple truth is that, unless you are a model or happen to look like one, providing the men or women who will be browsing your ad with a likeness of you will be a great boon for them (who doesn't prefer to screen out potential dates who may not meet the "minimum appearance requirement"?) but of little benefit to you. Playing fast and loose with photographs subjects you to the same set of superficial criteria that jinx our face-to-face encounters. If you're a picture-perfect flirt, a photo op may be an advantage—unless, of course, you prefer to found your relationships on a less physical basis. If your unique charms don't always manifest themselves on film, you may find that you are being passed over for more showy candidates.

I suggest that you wait to exchange photos until some measurable mutual interest between you and your responders has been established. And I prefer to delay the photo trade until any new friend and I have established an ongoing "snail mail" (via the U.S. postal service) correspondence. Why do I insist on the pen pal bit, when e-mail is so simple? Because I have found that a man who is willing to physically write a letter, put it in an envelope, stamp it and carry it to a mailbox or post office is a man who is willing to undergo some inconvenience to get to know me better. In other words, he is demonstrating that he is somewhat serious about me—and in a real-world sense. Another reason I like to exchange letters with my prospects is that it allows me to separate the readers and writers from those who can only interact via a relatively illiterate media. (E-mail is great but emoticons are hardly the language of love.)

The bottom line is this: Any 'net acquaintance who finds you charming before you have sent a picture is more likely to find you charming after you send one. And isn't that the very best of what internet flirtation has to offer?

DEVELOPING RESPONSE-ABILITY

"I placed my ad yesterday . . . and while I was browsing the site I found the most wonderful woman!" gushed Alan, the national sales manager for a major airline.

I asked Alan what distinguished this special woman from the pack.

"Well, she's just the right age and she's a buyer for a huge department store so she's solvent, unlike my last girlfriend. But she isn't all work and no play. She's musical. She plays the clarinet in a jazz band. She's athletic—she runs about fifteen miles a week. And can you believe it, she lives in Columbus, Ohio!"

I was tempted to crack out the smelling salts. Columbus was a city Alan traveled to often on business. Since Alan's demanding job made it difficult for him to meet and court women in his own hometown, Ms. Perfect had just handed him an opportunity to combine business travel with pleasure. Now Alan was so excited, he seemed in danger of hyperventilation. Without pausing long enough to even take a breath, he continued to catalog the ideal woman's many qualifications, until I held my finger to his lips.

"I understand that you feel she's all that and a bag of chips," I interrupted. "But what I want to know is, did you write to her?"

Suddenly Alan was dumbstruck. "Are you kidding? What would I *say*?"

There is something about responding to a well-written personal ad that gives even an otherwise effusive, poetic, Thomas Pynchon—esque writer pause. The author of the ad (if he or she has followed my guidelines) seems so dynamic, busy, interesting and together, surely he or she will receive an avalanche of responses. Meanwhile, there sits the prospective responder, in broken-in flannel pajamas, microwavable TV dinner tray in hand, looking like a painting entitled *Still Life with Drudgery*, wondering how to distinguish his or her response letter from the rest. Actually, it is easier than you think.

Of all the ways to flirt available on the 'net, personal ads are my preferred way to go. In the last two years, I have received literally thousands of responses from men all over the world. Many have evolved into very rewarding internet friendships; others into important professional connections; still others into very memorable dates and continuing relationships from New York to Australia. While I cannot begin to unravel the mystery of romantic "chemistry," or how to create it, I can certainly tell you what hits home for me in a successful personal ad response.

First and foremost, I like a response that lets me know that my ad has been read with attention. This means that your response should include commentary on any mutual interests, mention of any shared values or experiences and, most of all, affirmation of any romantic desires or goals you may have in common. These simple references not only establish commonality (remember: People like people who are *like* them), but they reinforce the idea that at least one respondent (you!) has found the ad writer's personal data important enough to remember. And how flattering is that?

I also prefer to hear from respondents who are willing to go with the slow and easy flow of internet romance and not push for a quick resolution. Oh, sure, in business e-mail is the quickest, most efficient—and therefore, the least artful—method of communication. But in a romantic milieu, e-mail is heart-pounding, palm-moistening courtship's last, best hope. So take your time, enjoy the journey wherever it leads, and celebrate the romance of writing to this intriguing stranger. Communication leads to chemistry, and communication plus chemistry creates deep and meaningful intimacy. Use your correspondence as an opportunity to reveal yourself, and in so doing, to encourage others to reveal their most intimate selves. You'll increase your chances of making it to your new pen pal's short list. Rush it, push for a telephone number, an address or a face-to-face meeting, and you almost ensure that your response will be pushed aside.

Which reminds me: E-mail responses to a personal ad should be short and frequent, not the multi-page, eye-glazing opuses that overflow my electronic mailbox. Detail the traits that make you special but keep the story of your life to yourself. Someone you don't know yet will hardly be encouraged to get involved if they sense your life is all sturm und drang. Confess what inspired you to answer this particular ad but don't profess emotions you couldn't possibly feel. Insisting that you feel "like you've known each other forever" just makes you seem desperate, reckless or worse.

Dont rely on gimmicks to prompt a correspondent to write back. Virtual glasses of champagne (_/ _/) and roses (@}—>—>—) are de rigueur in some chat rooms but always make me wonder why I'm not worth the real thing when they show up in e-mail. Instead, send the internet address of a site that pertains to that special man or woman's favorite hobby or special interest. If she's wild for British soaps, turn her on to http://www.erols.com/brittv/. If he's a city boy and a window gardener, try http://www.garden-net.com. Or, better yet, just pretend you're a journalist interviewing a fascinating subject and ask some open-ended questions. People love to talk about themselves! They also tend to appreciate those who encourage them to do it.

Since men greatly outnumber women on the web, the male of the species may feel that he is at something of a disadvantage when it comes to writing a response that really commands attention. When the odds are against you, it is critical that you follow the guidelines above. That alone will keep you one step ahead of the competition. But to further enhance your chances you might try these additional suggestions. Remember, if your e-mail goes unread, you're hopes are dead!

• To get the best response, don't be the first response. The e-mail generated by a personal ad tends to come in a monumental early rush, then trickle off as time goes by. Needless to say, recipients tend to weed out the early returns heavily, often without even carefully reading them. When you see an interesting ad, wait a week or two before e-mailing. You will be less apt to be deleted with the earlier candidates.

• Avoid those conversational turn-offs that so often mar a man's ability to communicate. Can the one-upmanship. If she holds a yellow belt in Tae kwon do, don't brag about your brown one. Don't judge or criticize. If you don't love (or at least like) her, leave her alone. Keep the sexual comments and come-ons to yourself. And never, *ever* try to wheedle her into revealing her age or any other personal information she seems reticent about. No woman wants to be discriminated against because she's too old, too young or too in-between.

• If you're comfortable with the idea, send a photo. Might this ploy blow up in your face? It might . . . but sending a photo along with an introductory letter takes guts, and I, for one, appreciate a self-confident man. Besides, seeing your photo might motivate a less secure lady to send you hers, and things may progress faster once you've both seen the goods.

THERE'S NO PLACE LIKE HOME . . . FOR ROMANCE

One pleasant afternoon when I could have been outside enjoying the sun and sparkling (for New York City) air, I found myself in the depths of a dimly lit "cyber cafe," 'net surfing over my friend Peter's shoulder and extolling the virtues of web personal ads. While Peter searched for the site recently created as a companion to his favorite television show, *Personal FX: The Collectibles Show,* I told him that I was still receiving sixty responses every week to the ad I'd placed with Cupidnet in April 1996.

I expected Peter to be impressed. Instead, he just nodded blankly and mumbled, "Yeah, I get a lot of mail, too."

My friend was obviously not getting the importance of what I was trying to tell him. So I went on to explain that I had not only "met" these men electronically, I had arranged to spend time with several of them face to face in my hometown or theirs. I further confessed that I had found two of my e-friends to be quite compatible, and that I was planning to meet with them again in the near future.

After that ringing endorsement, I felt sure that Peter and I would spend the rest of the day composing an ad for him. But he never looked up from his work.

"Yeah, it's fun to meet new people," he mumbled vacantly. "I've met . . . well, I dunno . . . maybe a dozen or so. In a couple of months."

That was all I could stand. I grabbed Peter by his lapels and forced him to confront me eye to eye. "Okay. You've made your 'you've got mail' notification voice hoarse from overuse. You've met a dozen new women in just a few weeks. Well, you may be a great guy with a magnetic personality, Peter, but just what are you up to?"

Peter shrugged. "I am totally into UFOs and collecting evidence of visitors from other planets. So I created my own homepage," my friend explained. "It took some work and a little research, but my site has gotten twelve thousand hits in the last four months!"

"And the mail?" I urged, eager to get in on the act, too.

"At the end of text I ask for comments, and nearly half of my visitors drop me an e-mail. Of those, about thirty percent are female." Peter grinned. "It's like having a little flirting factory running full steam twenty-four hours a day. It makes contacts for me when I'm at work, when I'm at the gym and after I've gone to sleep. I'm an absentee flirt, Susan! What could be better?"

What could be better, indeed? Business isn't my thing, but the business of romance certainly is. After a few minutes with Peter I decided that I could be a very motivated captain of industry if I had a flirting factory steaming along in the background while I worked on my seminars and books! But isn't creating a homepage incredibly complicated?

I am pleased to report that it is not. Simple, step-by-step programs that make setting up an attractive, graphically interesting homepage easy enough for the casual computer user (and flirt) are widely available. Moreover, your homepage doesn't have to be extremely showy or cutting edge to attract wave after wave of 'net surfers. If it is well thought out, informative, amusing, or if the text simply puts a fresh perspective on a popular subject, your homepage will almost certainly attract attention. But will taking the time to create a page, or hiring an expert to design a page for you, reap cyberdating dividends? It will if you consider Peter's guidelines when building a "flirting factory" of your own:

Capitalize on your interests and hobbies. Peter is a great guy with wit so dry it could ruin the tourist trade at Niagara Falls. Nevertheless, Peter's personality is not enough to attract and entertain large numbers of browsers. That's why, when Peter began searching for an expansive, endlessly fascinating homepage topic, he looked to the heavens—and to his interest in UFOs.

UFOs have always been a hot topic with a burgeoning, zealous, predominantly male audience, but with the popularity of *The X-Files* and other related films and programs, Peter suspected that an informational site compiling evidence of UFO sightings would attract more women in his age range than ever. He was right. Although his was a relatively small site, he was inundated with responses. Now he spends his time exchanging e-mail with women and men who share his passion.

And what if your area of interest isn't quite as current, popular or sought after as Peter's? It may still be worth your while to create a homepage! I recently met a woman named Robin who is fascinated with Norwegian folk dancing. Her homepage has attracted only those special singles who share her fairly narrow field of interest, yet it has netted her several ongoing contacts.

The truth is, the success of a homepage cannot be measured by the amount of e-mail it generates. A site can only be considered successful if it puts you in touch with the *kind* of partner you desire.

If your goal is to meet that *one* special person, it is the quality of response you get that matters, not the quantity.

Register your site at search engines. A search engine is an enormous database that enables internet users to search for and find information by typing in one or more keywords. Yahoo, Alta Vista, Excite, Netfind, Webcrawler, Lycos and Infoseek are examples of search engines. Each search engine offers the creators of newly established homepages a form by which they can register the URL (uniform resource locator) of the new site. Registration takes minutes, and once completed, it ensures that anyone searching for information on your website's topic will be directed to your homepage.

Maintain a guest book. When well-bred Victorians paid a social call to a special man or woman, they left an engraved calling card used to signal their interest and encourage reciprocal contact. By providing the surfers who visit your homesite with a guest book to sign, you send a message that you are open to communication from those who share your interests. You even supply a convenient forum for correspondence. But if a guest book seems too complicated a programming endeavor to you, simply add a line near the end of your page that reads something like: "I hope you have enjoyed visiting my homepage. I would love to hear your comments and questions. Please e-mail me at . . ." then fill in an e-mail address. (The unexpected mail generated by a popular homepage can overflow a virtual mailbox, so I would recommend setting up an e-mail address just for these responses.) It is also interesting to keep a record of just how many visitors your homepage attracts, so you might consider setting up a counter like Peter did.

Try to include some frequently searched references. You don't have to be a rocket scientist to know that a site that includes widely known, popular references such as jazz, gardening, cooking, fitness or Antonio Banderas is going to get more hits than one that includes such references as neurolinguistics, pvc pipe, blubber and its many uses, and the like. As fascinating as these topics may be, these subjects simply aren't searched as often as topics that appeal to the "common denominator."

Peter knew his subject would attract those women who were surfing the most current wave of interest in UFOs. Chances are that one of your hobbies or interests will attract just as much attention. So work it, honey! Just don't throw in gratuitous references that will make your site a search engine mainstay, then fail to include information on that topic. I was never so angry as the day I looked up a specific town in the Berkshires, clicked on what seemed to be an informative and touristy site, and found myself instead in a homepage conceived by married "swingers." The site told me too much I didn't want to know and not enough that I did. And I left an e-mail saying just that, too.

Join a ring. If you have been exploring the internet at all, no doubt you have already experienced the convenience of surfing à la "ring." A ring is a virtual guided tour of similar sites that have been linked together to form a circular, informational route. Getting your site added to an existing ring is a great way to direct hundreds of fascinating new people to your homepage.

Ring sites are pages that are similar in type or share a common topic. They are also linked by a button that appears at the bottom of each page that, when clicked, automatically sends the surfer to the next site on the ring "tour." In my travels, I have discovered rings on a wide variety of topics, including authors' rings, readers' rings, women's interests rings, rings maintained by people who suffer from the same conditions or diseases, Spice Girls fans' rings, anti–Spice Girls (and nearly every other performer) rings, professional musicians' rings (organized by instrument), and rings devoted to now-defunct television shows, musical groups and movies, many of which nonetheless still enjoy what is commonly referred to as a "cult following." (Want to have some ghoulish fun on a cyberdate? Explore the *Dark Shadows* ring! It's a site you'll really be able to sink your teeth into.)

It isn't difficult to make your homepage a web ring stop. Simply contact the "ringmaster" at www.webring.org and you'll discover everything you need to know to join a ring or start your own. Who knows . . . this may not be the last ring in your future.

Share a little information about yourself. How many times have you found yourself engrossed in a particularly unique, funny or inspirational site and suddenly you sit back and think, "Who did this? And why? What inspired this site's designer? And most of all, is he or she single?"

Every homepage functions like a Rorschach test. No matter how scholarly its tone, no matter how glossy its graphics, it invariably reveals some compelling truths about its creator's perspective. Since all of my readers are attractive, considerate, fascinating flirts, why not prepare for that contingency by providing the curious men and women who visit your website with a little background information? You can safely reveal details like your first name and your general location. (I've always been tempted to offer a bit of warmth to hardy men from Alaska and Maine—and I am not alone.) A sentence or two detailing how you came to be interested in your homepage subject will make you seem more human and approachable. And as for your marital status, be sure to include the fact that you are looking! Notice of your eligibility will breeze right by browsers who are happily wed, but single people are certain to take note. Nature abhors a vacuum. Don't be surprised if more than a few naturally charming surfers rush to fill the vacancy in your life.

REV UP YOUR SEARCH ENGINES

Seek and ye shall find a personals site to suit every available person. But just to make certain you're hearing from every possible Romeo or Juliet who shares your interests, why not set up a homepage where he or she can find you? And when you do, consider these tips:

• "Are you hot for a cool Canadian?" (and I am not making this up) is not the kind of salutation I like to see in a response to my ad, and most of the women I know feel the same. Your conversational partner is more likely to warm up to you if you focus your attention on his or her feelings rather than your own.

• If you suffer from a case of what eminent psychologist Albert Ellis calls LFT (Low Frustration Tolerance), those singles sites that are difficult to read, confusing to navigate, illogically designed, too esoteric or simply overstimulating will certainly leave you cold. Don't miss an opportunity to flirt because of some programmer's poor planning! Try a smaller, more manageable place to publish your ad.

• Set aside a few hours to get acquainted with the hottest sites. You'd spend an evening checking out a trendy new singles club, wouldn't you? Then give the virtual hot spots equal time. I spent several hours familiarizing myself with the web before I felt confident enough to get acquainted with the natives.

• Virtual bouquets, greeting cards, musical tributes are a nice thought but can be a pain to pick up. If they're simple to collect (i.e., if they can be retrieved just by clicking on a link) great. Otherwise, find a less gimmicky way to get noticed.

• Before you register your homepage, make sure there's a *there* there. A site that promises information on a pet subject then doesn't deliver is a waste of time. It is also an irritation, and anger doesn't put anyone in the mood to flirt.

Last but not least—

• If you're unattached and looking, say so! The singles I know are so tired of the romantically ambivalent, the chronically "unready" and all the other "Who-Me? Advertise?" commitment-phobes, they'd give their left ring finger to meet someone who is actually looking for love and unafraid to say so. If you're in search of a lasting partnership, state your case in your personal ad. If you're ready to trade in your standing reservation for a table for one, mention it in your homepage bio. Even love-starved men and women aren't going to offer to join you if they believe your table is already filled.

7
Do You Want to Go Somewhere a Little More Private?

I met Lise, a woman of about 35, at a "fence nailing party" thrown by a charity whose members build affordable housing for low-income families. Lise was there as part of a corporate contingent that had contributed hundreds of volunteer hours to the project. I was there to pound a few nails. As far as I could tell, Lise couldn't have cared less about me. She wasn't particularly interested in my connection to the charity, my attempts at conversation or my nailing ability. But when she learned that I was currently writing a book on cyberflirtation, she reacted with a shriek.

"Cyberflirting? I had the *worst* experience flirting on the 'net!" she exclaimed. "It was disappointing, it was confusing, it was frustrating, but worst of all, it nearly got me fired!"

Though the party—and the hammers—were now in full swing, Lise had my complete attention. "Tell me about it," I urged, as if Lise could be suppressed.

From the time Lise was granted web access through the company she worked for, she was fascinated with the 'net. She loved the idea of electronic travel and spent every free moment visiting sites all over the world. She communicated with colleagues from Antwerp to Zagreb. And in her free moments, she frequented the chats.

Lise was a true professional. She knew full well that flirting on the job was risky business. Nevertheless, in time, she became so engrossed in the chats that she would stay late on Friday nights just so she could take advantage of the increased numbers of available men who signed on after 7 p.m. . . . until she met George.

"Some men have to grow on you, but I felt a connection to George right away," Lise revealed. And George seemed to share Lise's sense of intimacy. They chatted easily from the start, exchanging their more private thoughts through a series of good-natured IMs while they each maintained a presence in the chat room. The next day when Lise checked her e-mail, she found a charming message from George. He had added her to his "buddy list." She didn't mind.

Lise and George chatted once more before George suggested that they meet for a "private chat" in a room just for two. Since Lise felt a strong kinship with her new friend, and since her first impressions of others rarely failed her, she accepted his invitation without hesitation. She was only in the room a few seconds when it became clear that the man she was meeting this time wasn't the George she felt she knew.

"He was like a different person," Lise told me, still incredulous after many months. "Instead of being courteous and playful and almost courtly, as he had been in the chat rooms, he was pushy and insistent. He demanded my address so he could meet me. When I refused to reveal it, he asked for my phone number so he could call me. Though I considered giving him my business number, I decided against it, and it's a very good thing I did. George tried to engage me in cybersex, and began to describe what struck me as a very kinky and frightening sexual scenario. I signed off immediately, but that didn't stop George. He was so angry, he e-mailed nearly all of the executives in the company I worked for—their e-mail addresses were right there on the corporate homepage—telling them that I was using my company computer to solicit sexual contacts!

"I explained to everyone who would listen what really happened but, of course, I was completely humiliated," Lise divulged. "My internet access disappeared that day. And so did my ability to trust my instincts about the people I meet."

Lise shrugged. "After a couple of chat room conversations, I believed I knew George. It turned out I didn't know him at all."

The fact is, no matter how long you've been chatting or exchanging e-mail, no matter what you have done to "check out" a new friend's story, you don't really know your internet pals, either. Although the internet has brought together millions of honest, straightforward people, it is also a haven for countless liars, cheats (marital and otherwise), swindlers and cyberjerks of every imaginable stripe, kink and description. In other words, when you meet a man or woman who seems too good to be true, he or she probably is. And even if people are being completely honest and all of the details they have shared about their stellar career, bucolic lifestyle, dazzling looks and profound sensitivity are absolutely true, it is impossible to guess at what they have chosen *not* to tell you. Or even which little white lies about a pen friend's qualities or motives you have effectively told yourself.

Told *yourself*? That's right. Unless Mr. or Ms. Almost-Right is unnaturally secure and forthright and absolutely committed to providing you with a warts-and-all portrait, the man or woman with whom you have been communicating has almost certainly made an effort to put the best possible face on your image of him or her. (Do you think my personal ads contain any reference to my laugh lines? Do you think my friend Dan has even once revealed in a chat room that he has eaten nothing but Chinese take-out for the last 237 nights in a row? Get real.) Using phrases from his or her e-mail or chat conversations, you begin to build a fantasy of him or her in your mind. Make no mistake about it: The fantasy is created entirely from your own imagination, bolstered by bits of information you have hand-selected and chosen to accept. In fact, where no information exists, you may even have projected it. Before you know it, you, like Lise and innumerable other hopeful, optimistic singles, have conjured up a relationship based solely on your desire for intimacy, and a glowing image of a complete stranger that he or she may be hard-pressed to live up to in the real world.

The only real relationship is one that can make it in the real world. I have studied the way human beings communicate—verbally and nonverbally—for more than twenty-five years. In my opinion, you can never really know a person until you actually meet and become "real" to each other as quirky, complex individuals and, perhaps, as a couple. Of course, there are serious risks in taking a relationship off-line. We read about those all the time in the newspapers. It is critical, therefore, that you get to know your 'net friend as well as you possibly can, screen to screen, before you arrange to meet face to face.

You can begin that process in a private chat room, a cozy little forum-for-two that offers a little more one-on-one communication, encourages a little more intimacy and provides a viable meeting ground between cyberspace and the real world.

PRIVATE CHATS

Private chats are a great place to get to know a person a little better without going all the way and inviting him or her to meet your cat . . . or your mother.

Your mission for now, should you choose to accept it, is to crank up your relationship just a notch. (See my suggestions about cybersex, below.) I've found that using the private chat room the same way I would a neighborhood coffee shop—as a casual, non-threatening locus for two people who wish to explore common ground—makes it easy to develop healthy intimacy without adding a heavy sexual or overwhelming romantic component to what is a very fragile relationship.

Of course, there is an undeniably romantic component to this scenario. The very act of inviting a special someone to a private chat suggests that you have picked him from the bunch, that you value her input enough to want to hear more, that you feel so at ease with him that you are willing to take a small risk to add a bit more spontaneity and honesty to the mix. A touch of romance is not a bad thing. Indeed, it's the reason for this book. But romantic infatuation only intensifies any fantasy you may be harboring of the idealized partner, and an unrealistic approach can lead to poor judgment and ill-advised meetings. Your job then, in this private chat, is to discover as much as you can about a man or woman who has impressed you in the chats or personals, and to see whether he or she is just as likely to impress you in person.

And that isn't always easy. Meeting a person in a private chat is like arranging an assignation in the isolation chamber of the local sanitarium. There is no external stimuli in the room that might hurt you—no yammering chatters, no IMs from desperate strangers, no "terms of agreement"–defying kvetchers—but there is nothing that might help communication along, either. There are, for example, no political speechifiers to critique, no chat room crazies to comment upon and no blatant liars to discover. (Liar identification is a favorite chat room activity.) In short, you and your chosen one will be two people in a room full of nothing. It is possible that without the chaos of external stimulation you may find absolutely nothing to talk about.

To offset that possibility and to enhance your chances of finding out as much as possible about the man or woman who has inspired this tête-à-tête, I suggest that you come to the private chat with a prepared list of what you want to learn about your internet companion. If you are already feeling emotionally attached to or lascivious about the person in question, make sure you compose your list in a moment of clarity, or ask an objective friend to help. I have a friend who believed she had found her soul mate in a man she "picked up" at an on-line trivia game. Having just unloaded a chronically unfaithful real-life beau, she was ready to pack her bags and run to her "e-male's" arms, until I casually asked her what his last name was. Admitting that she didn't know brought her to her senses. She knew so little about this man. Why was she so willing to give up so much? (P.S.: She came to understand that when you're on the rebound is the worst possible time to play the cyberflirtation game. She stayed home and took a sabbatical from the web until she got over it.)

Of course, you must not allow your chat to take on the tone of an interview, or worse, an interrogation. Be your most charming self! Be free with playful banter but always reflect the focus of the conversation back to your partner's favorite subject: him- or herself. Keep restating your date's statements in the form of a question ("You say you have every afternoon free? In this lovely weather? Your job hours must be flexible. Does your job take you outdoors?") and follow up with a lot of open-ended questions. You won't have to fish for information long before you get a sense of whether this one is a keeper or an undeveloped specimen you'll want to throw back into the pond.

And how much personal information should you share? Though I certainly know singles who reveal everything from their bodice-ripping romantic history to their addresses and telephone numbers at this stage, I tend to keep my most personal data to myself. Even if I have been chatting with a man for several weeks, even if I have shared a private room with him more than once, I am still vividly aware that my conversational partner is a relative stranger, that all I can possibly base my judgment of him on is his word and his word is a commodity that has yet to prove its worth. Since those are the irrefutable facts of the matter, I keep him at arm's length, the way I would any stranger. I reveal my current status (single, looking, interested in relationship and friendship) but not my innermost feelings. I disclose my neighborhood but not my address (unless it is a post office box). I offer a business telephone number but not a personal one. (Your fax line or a separate number you have installed for computer use will do nicely.) Most of all, I answer his questions honestly, even when I suspect that my answers may constitute "deal breakers" for him. If, at the private chat stage, he is asking about my weight, my age, how many children I have and what ages they are, whether I work, my religious affiliation, etc., it is because he is using this information to weed out those women he likes but whom he considers to be unsuitable for him. When you are asked similar questions, my advice to you is *do not lie.* His deal-breaker issues may seem superficial to you but they are important to him. They are also unlikely to change. So get over any idea that he'll accept you—extra thirty pounds and all—when he meets you face to face. He'll feel that you've wasted his time, and he won't give you the chance to waste any more.

You will note that, although I don't hesitate to compliment, I do not share any information about my "feelings" toward my new friend. There are two reasons for that. First, I am a very visual and intuitive person and as such, I do not believe I could experience a significant emotional link with anyone I have not met. Second, I simply feel that too many single surfers approach with heart in hand, too willing to believe that this is certainly *the one*—and too quick to confess that feeling to others. Such professions of love, lust or whatever emotion you happen to be professing only throw a fledgling relationship off-balance. To ensure that my flirtations are without serious intent and to keep the communication playful, I maintain my silence about any sexual or romantic fantasies I may be harboring. And I always mention to my conversational partner, as nonchalantly as possible, that I have every intention of getting to know any other interesting singles I may encounter on my web travels. This maneuver not only keeps him from getting too involved with me (or his fantasy of me), it also allows me to experience his reaction. A burst of anger or envy tells me a great deal about his motives and psychological stability.

It should also go without saying that I never ever allow a private chat to metamorphose into a setting for cybersex. There is nothing sexier than your fantasy of the exciting man or woman you've been burning up the lines with. And why shouldn't it be arousing to you? You created it using all of the images and sensory cues that are most titillating to you! But cybersex between people who have become friends can derail any possibility that you will ever become more. For one thing, it forces too much sexual intimacy before you have had a chance to establish an emotional bond. Or it can cause one of you to experience great embarrassment and make further communication impossible. Or it can bring up a real disparity between you and your partner. You might learn, for instance, that what constitutes intimacy for you is just "a physical thing" to him . . . a situation that can't end in anything but hard feelings. My readers know my favorite line is if sex is on your mind, keep it out of the chat room. There is plenty of time for physical exploration when you've gotten to know each other better, and when you are physically in the same place. Try the Cyrano approach. Write great letters.

Other than these possible pitfalls, is there a downside to the private chat? The only problem I have found is that a private chat may not be an option if you and your conversational partner do not share the same server. In that case, what is a cyberflirt to do? Simple! Just surf on in to my absolute favorite relationship-expanding option.

THE VIRTUAL DATE

"What I hate is that staged feeling," a young flirt told me after a session of my School of Flirting®. "I mean, asking a woman to join you in a private chat room is so . . . obvious. It's like you're inviting her up to see your etchings."

Staged? Two people who hardly know each other communing mentally but not physically in a room full of nothing? Does that seem staged to you? It certainly might! Real-life first encounters don't take place in a vacuum but in a vibrant world filled with sights and sounds and the scent of a man's aftershave and wonderful flavors like the taste of a fresh white raspberry pavlova for two. If the fates (and both of you) are willing, that vigorous and sensate world is precisely where you will ultimately come together. But if you're still uncomfortable with how little you do—and how much you don't—know about each other and you'd like to get to know each other a little better, there may be no more nearly real way to do so than to go on a virtual date.

Just what is a virtual date? And should you stick a virtual quarter-for-the-phone under your mouse just in case it doesn't work out? Forget it . . . it can't fail! A virtual date is an agreement between two people to simultaneously visit the same website and, as they explore the site, to communicate their thoughts, impressions and especially their silliest comments via instant message—just as they would if they were visiting a real-world hot spot.

And where can one go on a virtual date? Literally anywhere in the world and beyond! Oh, sure, an evening at the local bistro can give you a "taste" of the Paris of Edith Piaf, but in a matter of minutes on the web you and a companion can tour the Louvre, learn to prepare crêpes suzette the classic way, get a front-row-seat view of the hottest couture shows and listen to the real Edith Piaf sing her trademark "La Vie en Rose" so powerfully you'd swear you can smell the characteristic smokiness in her voice. Women, adventure dates help men bond. Travel to the Amazon or scale Everest (okay, go sailing, it's safer).

With a universe of destinations limited only by your imagination and the speed of your modem, choosing one can be a bit overwhelming. (This isn't like selecting one movie among the twelve playing at the local multiplex.) That's why I prefer to take my direction from among the many sites that might enhance whatever common ground my companion and I share. If we both love art, I might whisk him off to see the Sistine Chapel . . . or the fabulous Art of Motorcycles exhibit at guggenheim.com. The "tour" will entertain me, and give me an idea of whether his idea of art leans more toward the ridiculous or the sublime. If my new friend is deeply involved with a hobby, I might send him a link to a site he'll love and suggest that we visit it together. It never fails to impress him, and best of all it gives me the chance to see if he impresses me.

Unlike an actual date where you can find yourself stuck with a dud or a bill, the virtual date is a win-win situation. Even if you find out that what she described as a "dry sense of humor" seems more like sarcasm to you, even if you discover that his propensity for multisyllabic communication—a trait that so charmed you in the chats—now seems a trifle ostentatious, you'll still come away from the experience knowing more than you did before about a subject that interests you. You'll also become incredibly "well-traveled." I've been to more fascinating, far-flung places on virtual dates than I can possibly visit in real life, from the Tower of London to the pyramids at Giza. And I've taken in all kinds of sights from the jewels of Tsarist Russia to the latest in home fitness equipment. (When in doubt, go shopping!) For your convenience I've listed some ideas as to the kinds of places you might go on your virtual date in the last chapter of this book. Just remember to absorb a bit more information about your date than you do about the sharks of Asia, Polish poster art or any other scintillating subject.

CLOSE ENCOUNTERS

A recent transplant to Manhattan, 29-year-old Marnie was a busy young executive for a media conglomerate. Her job fulfilled a lot of her dreams, but working seventy-plus hours a week made it impossible for her to search for a dream man to share the benefits of her career. When she began to reach out for companionship over the internet, her friends were relieved . . . that is, until Marnie found a man she wanted to meet face to face.

"You would think that I had agreed to go for chili with Mephistopheles himself," Marnie told me. "All of a sudden the friends who had been so supportive were absolutely aghast. They were calling me at all hours saying things like, 'You don't even know this person!' 'He says he likes the quiet life? Could that mean he's in solitary confinement?' And my personal favorite: 'What do you mean he's probably very nice? If he's looking for dates on the 'net, something must be wrong with him!' "

Six months later, Marnie's friends have finally come to accept that cyberflirtation really works. Her web friend, Matt, has visited several times and the relationship is going strong. Marnie has also gotten acclimated to her high-powered job and has begun to date but Matt remains a part of her life. Thanks to her PC and the willingness to take a calculated risk, she's made what may be a lasting connection.

The chums on your softball team may have been panting for daily updates on your 'net-sploits with SheeRa from Cleveland or SweeTPi (she's a mathematician) from Alabama. Your girlfriends may have been downright nosy about your internet adventures, full of questions about each man's "qualifications" and anxiously pricing personal computers of their own so you could turn them on to the chat rooms and personals sites that have been so entertaining and socially stimulating for you. But just announce that you intend to relocate your relationship with one of the compatible singles you have met from on-line to off and these very people will be the first to tell you that you've already *gone* off . . . your rocker!

It doesn't matter how intriguing, fun, meaningful, open or free of serious intent an on-line relationship might be. Nor does it matter how benign, playful, innocent or inconsequential your real-life chums have judged it to be. The minute you announce that an internet liaison has made the leap from your computer screen to your appointment book, the warnings begin. Don't you know that everyone on the internet is a geek/social outcast/weirdo/potential predator? Aren't you afraid a casual contact might rob you and rape you and leave you for dead? How could you risk life and limb to spend time with who-knows-who from who-knows-where?

How silly! And how hypocritical. Take a close look at the naysayers. Aren't these the same men who wouldn't think twice about leaving a party with a woman they have known for perhaps ten minutes? Aren't these the women who wouldn't think twice about meeting that friendly stranger they met on the bus for a quick lunch, or inviting that cute fellow dog-owner to join them for a walk in the park? So why are they making a mountain out of your molehill of e-mail? They could be jealous, particularly if you've accumulated more names in your computer address book than they have in their little black books. Your friends might be techno-phobes who are suspicious of any media you plug into the wall—and into your life. Or they could be frightened by the shocking stories of internet romance-gone-wrong that have made their way into the headlines, though these stories are few and far between relative to the number of people who meet on the 'net every day.

The fact is, every first date has its risks. But those risks are the same whether you are meeting a man you first bumped into on the web or a woman you encountered over a fallen crab soufflé at a dinner party.

Dan Bender, the president of Cupid's Network, which bills itself as the "world's largest network of romantic eligibles on the 'net," met his wife, Nancy, on the 'net. And he sums up the safety issues this way: "The media likes to portray on-line dating as something very dangerous. In reality, the opposite is true. It's like flying on an airline: Accidents do occur, but very rarely. In fact, flying is safer than driving. So it goes with on-line dating. If cyberdaters take their time and follow basic commonsense precautions, then the chances of meeting an ax murderer are virtually eliminated." My own experiences reinforce Dan's assertion. I have enjoyed in-person meetings with on-line acquaintances from coast to coast and on several continents and I have never experienced any difficulty. And neither will you, if you simply follow a few common-sense guidelines.

First, if you are from different geographical regions, compromise on a mutually agreeable, neutral place for your meeting. A spot that is neither your-place-nor-mine ensures that you will meet as equals, with equal veto power. The trials of affecting a compromise will also tip you off as to just how far your new friend is willing to go—literally and figuratively—to get to know you better. Are you a twenty-five-mile adventure? Or a 100+ mile investment? You'll know before you leave home.

I also suggest that you keep your initial meeting brief—and that you make sure to meet in public. As I have said before, I meet many of my internet pen pals when I travel. Since some men still think of a woman traveler as lonely and unfulfilled, with unlimited leisure time to fill, I make sure to let my new acquaintance know that I will be busy, that I will set aside an hour or two to meet with him, and that I will meet him at a restaurant, gallery or other public place convenient to my hotel. I do not allow him to pick me up for the date or take me anywhere in his car. If the first meeting goes well, I can always make another date for another day. If it does not, either of us can say thank you, nice to meet you, and bow out gracefully.

In terms of the conversation, try to steer your interaction into the real world. It can be very tempting for two people who don't know each other very well to relive their on-line experiences, to gossip about other chat room pals and to keep their relationship to within the limitations of the monitor screen. Common ground is comforting but a relationship that wallows in the past is a relationship without a future. This is your opportunity to create shared experiences. Take advantage of it!

If, at any time during the rendezvous, you begin to sense a gap between what you believed to be true about your new friend and the evidence before you, if you feel pressured or manipulated, if you experience that ineffable feeling that something is wrong (children describe this as the "uh-oh feeling"), don't make nice-nice.

Make tracks. Human beings, like every other animal, are imbued with a sixth sense that warns them of impending danger. I urge you to trust it. Experience has taught me to honor mine.

And in the event that bells ring and rockets go off, make sure that a red flag goes up, too. Chemistry can be intense, but it doesn't make up for the fact that this person remains a virtual stranger. Stick to your schedule. (If you have told him that you have limited time to spend with him, end the date at the preordained hour. You can use the extra time to "cool off.") And stick to your guns. If the plan is to meet for a casual drink, don't invite her for dinner. Don't invite him to your hotel room. Don't even feel you must make her a part of your other weekend activities. Allowing yourself to be "swept away" will only cloud your perception. And bear in mind that what you perceive as "closeness" may be too close for that special someone to handle. He or she has a comfort zone, too. Respect it.

Most of all, if this twosome turns out to be gruesome, don't give up! Too many singles suffer one disappointment and turn their backs on cyberflirting altogether. But why? If the next woman you met at a dance two-stepped all over your ego, would you hang up your shoes forever? If the next man who chatted you up at the neighborhood pizza joint suffered from delusions, would you swear off pepperoni? Of course not! So place another ad . . . visit a new chat . . . establish a presence at that NASCAR message board you bypassed on your last virtual date. The possibilities are endless as long as you don't end them.

HOW WELL DO YOU KNOW HIM/HER ANYWAY?

Let's face it: You can meet a louse, a fraud, a nut, a cheat and even a sicko just about anywhere: in the produce aisle of the grocery store, answering phones at a telethon, even, inadvertently, through your mother! ("Have I got a guy for you! Let me tell you about my friend Edna's cousin's sister's boy. . . .") But you'll be much less likely to meet one through your internet connection if you ask yourself these questions before arranging another late-night chat, or that important first date.

1. Make a list of every fact you know about this person: his real name, his age, his physical type, his profession, etc. Now make a list of every fact you know about a casual real-life acquaintance; a girl you speak with while waiting for the apartment building elevator, or the friendly check-out guy at the video store. How do the two lists compare?

2. Refer to your lists of facts again. Ask yourself how you know these facts. Are these things he has told you? How many of them are details that you might have surmised, assumed or projected? (You may be fleshing out an incomplete story with wishful thinking.) How do the facts he has provided jibe with his profile? How do they stand up against details he revealed during chat sessions?

3. Is her personality the same from chat session to chat session? Is she sometimes moody, paranoid, overly sensitive or forgetful? Could she be hiding a drug or alcohol problem?

4. Is his schedule flexible? Is he available to chat at your convenience or is he unavailable nights, weekends or holidays? Cybercreeps are notoriously forgetful when it comes to revealing certain information. Could he have "forgotten" to mention his wife and three children in his personal ad? Or the fact that he spends every other weekend in jail? (Impossible? Oh, I could name names!) Or is your internet acquaintance signed-on nearly all the time? Is he able to interact with others in real-life, or is he only an on-screen personality?

5. How much do you know about her family/personal life? Did she pull you in by revealing a personal drama or problem? It is dangerous to become involved with a drama queen— particularly one you really don't know.

6. In what areas does he express the most curiousity about you? Does he want to know your dreams? Learn about your lifestyle? Does he want to know what kind of books or films you like? Or does he ask the most questions about how you invest your money?

7. Has she expressed a desire to meet your friends, male and female? Has he suggested that you bring a friend along on any first date you plan, just to make you feel more comfortable and secure? A man or woman who is willing to meet those

who care about you most is a person who is unafraid of scrutiny.

8. If circumstances made you late for a chat or if you missed the chat altogether, how did she react? Was he angry toward you? Did she express suspicion concerning your whereabouts? Did you feel that you *had* to explain?

9. Is he willing to put in the time to allow this relationship to develop? Or is he pushing for a phone number, address, face-to-face encounter or cybersex?

10. Does she have an uncanny knack for knowing when to instant message you, or has she added you to her buddy list without your permission? Does he have a remarkable tendency to "pop up" in just the chats you're visiting, or is he using a locater to track your movements?

An inauspicious answer to any of these questions should give you pause—and a thoughtful pause will give you plenty of time to decide whether to proceed with the relationship or not. And whatever the answers, don't go to his or her apartment for your first meeting.

Cyberflirtation can be wonderfully inventive, straightforward, romantic and *safe* if you heed the compliments as well as the possible cons, the warm-fuzzies as well as the warning signs.

8
The Virtual Broken-Hearts Club, and How Not to Join It

A relatively recent acquaintance, Jonathan, impressed me right away. Although he was quite young (he was just finishing up his degree in business and marketing), Jonathan was the most resourceful, practical and down-to-earth young man I had ever met. Not only was he pulling aces in his full-time course work, he held a demanding part-time job at a brokerage firm. In addition, Jonathan was active in student government, a bass player in an alternative rock band, a lively e-mail pal (all the best jokes were passed on to me by Jonathan) and a very successful flirt. I was shocked to learn, then, that Jonathan had been devastated by an on-line romance, and that he was resolute not ever to venture into the realm of cyberflirtation again.

"There's a place for everything on the internet: crossbow hunting, cross-dressing, mountain climbing, social climbing—you name it, it's there. But I'll tell you this," he continued wearily, "the World Wide Web is no place for love."

*   *   *

People are reluctant to give out a credit card number on-line. Why aren't they equally cautious when they give their hearts?

Cyberjerks are plentiful. So are the Don Juanitas who kiss and tell the whole chat room or singles site all the lurid details. And there are times when I am convinced that there are so many fibbers and cheaters on the web that there aren't enough scam artists left on the streets to make buying a moneybelt worthwhile.

Nevertheless, the internet *is* a great place to look for and find friendship, romance and love. The larger singles sites keep very credible records of the long-term romances and marriages they have fostered. And the friendships forged on the 'net are virtually innumerable, encompassing everything from casual acquaintances who share an interest or hobby to close confidants who could not pass a day without some sort of contact.

Of course, there is no such thing as flirtation without risk, and that doesn't change whether you're flirting at the local pub or in a public chat. But you can limit the emotional ante, increase your odds of romantic success and stay one step ahead of the virtual broken-hearts club membership committee if you navigate the on-line world with confidence, perspective and some basic information about what makes so many cyber-connections fail.

COMMON MISTAKES THAT MAKE ON-LINE ROMANCES CRASH

As Shakespeare so succinctly put it, "the course of true love never did run smooth." Of course, in the Bard's day the epitome of high-tech was a smoothly running guillotine. Now, on the cusp of the twenty-first century, we are more concerned with getting abruptly "cut off" by an internet server. And our computers have begun to play an active, nearly human role in our social lives.

"Therein lies the rub." The relationships that erupt when monitor meets monitor are, of course, susceptible to the same menu of pitfalls that have plagued relationships from time immemorial: jealousy, duplicity, cancellation due to lack of interest, the works. But they are also subject to a host of difficulties that are either created or exacerbated by computer interference, and these can make the course of internet romance considerably bumpier.

To keep your on-line relationship from "crashing," here are the problems you should watch for:

A false sense of intimacy. Late-night chats in the flickering and perhaps radioactive glow of the computer screen are conducive to romance, but they are also conducive to developing a false and potentially dangerous sense of intimacy between people who, in reality, hardly know each other.

Think about it. You're exchanging secrets. You're baring your soul. You're filling the screen with so many sweet nothings you don't dare lean too close for fear you'd stick. Aren't you investing a great deal of your inner self in a relationship with a person who calls himself "StudMuffN" and claims to be a single Chippendale's dancer but may or may not (to your knowledge) even be male? Before you spend another night passing up Letterman, Leno or a real-life friend for an impassioned heart-to-heart in cyberspace, I suggest a reality check. Stand outside a local restaurant or club until someone you know only by name strolls by. Ask yourself: Would you feel comfortable sharing the same depth of personal information with him? You undoubtedly would not. Yet, you've seen him in a number of contexts, made eye contact or shared some real contact. Don't you actually know more about this person than you do your internet Casanova?

Internet lovers are truly in a world of their own. The relationships on the computer screen exist in a vacuum, far from the reach of the real world. By filling this void with intimacies, you can make this realm seem real, but it is not. My advice? Keep it playful; banter, chat, *flirt*. But save your most personal secrets for someone you know personally.

Unrealistic expectations. If the way you perceive an e-pal make your hopes rise like a balloon, then unrealistic expectations will surely cause those hopes to erupt in your face.

Here's a case in point. I met a very lovely man through a personal ad I had placed at a singles site. Although the man was from another country, I knew I would be visiting his homeland soon, and I encouraged the relationship. After we had exchanged dozens of pieces of e-mail and shared several phone calls, I announced my travel plans and we agreed to meet off-line.

The date was everything I could have hoped it would be. He was intelligent, funny and charming . . . and more courtly than any other man I knew, until he took me home. Suddenly, the old-fashioned gentleman who had so thoughtfully pulled out my chair was pulling out every argument for allowing him in my room, and in my bed. When I remarked on the change in his manner, he looked at me, perplexed:

"Aren't you a flirting expert? And isn't sex what flirting is all about?" he demanded. "I just assumed . . ."

He assumed, did he? Well, to paraphrase *The Odd Couple*'s Felix Unger: Never assume, because when you assume, you make an "ass" of "u" and "me"! I explained to my escort that no profile or personal ad or e-mail description ever gives us a complete picture of an internet friend. I also told him that although it is human nature to imagine and "project" a fantasy of our own onto someone we hardly know, it makes a successful face-to-face encounter impossible. After all, how can you appreciate the person your cyberfriend really is if you're all hung up on the person you believe him or her to be?

When a totally groundless fantasy collides with cold, hard reality the result isn't pretty. Nor is the result flirtation. (Don't believe me? Just ask the man I described above.) Any on-line friend who seems too good to be true is, no doubt, just that. If you believe you've found the exception to that rule, you're kidding yourself . . . and deleting your chances of meaningful cyber-romance.

Vulgarity. Things were going swimmingly between me and another internet friend when he used a word for a part of the female anatomy that, I can assure you, he didn't learn in any medical text. His vocabulary turned me off completely—as it would most of the women I know—and I severed the connection then and there.

By the way, many men are just as put off by women who leer, insinuate, curse, post lurid messages and photos and indulge in other forms of vulgarity as women are by crude men. So if you're thinking about passing the latest adult e-jokes along to her, or if you're thinking of inviting him up to view the "artistic" photographs on your homepage, think again: Is this something you would feel comfortable sharing with a new aquaintance in a face-to-face situation? Is it suitable for polite society? If not, save it for those friends who know you well. They won't be wondering whether you are a pervert or a sexual predator.

Deception. I've seen cyber-romances overcome many things, from seemingly irreconcilable cultural differences (a Jewish science fiction writer and a Methodist minister? Who could have guessed that *that* would turn out to be a marriage made in heaven?) to great geographical hardship, but I have never *ever* seen one recover from a discovered deception.

Deception causes a classic lose-lose situation. If you are the one who has been caught in a lie, you lose your credibility with someone who might have been important to you. And because being found out is a singularly embarrassing situation—I mean, what's worth lying about? Your income? Your age? Whether your hair comes from a can?—you also risk eroding your self-esteem. If, on the other hand, you are the one who catches a new friend in a lie, you lose your willingness to trust that person. And because feeling that you've been "had" is so unsettling, you may also lose the ability to trust your own judgment.

Being discovered in even a relatively insignificant lie—regarding your birth date or job description, for example—throws into doubt everything you have ever said on any subject, whether it was said in sincerity or not. Being nabbed in a big lie—like denying you have a criminal record or a spouse—imbues you with all the synthetic charm of a Pinocchio, or Pinocchiette. Do you really expect a new, untried relationship to bounce back after a blow like that?

So stick to the script. Any line, story, embellishment or old-fashioned crock you pass on will almost certainly be revealed. Most of all, don't lie about your marital status. Spare us genuinely eligible singles the ten minutes it takes to notice that you are never available on-line on weekends or holidays, to discover why a single person like you drives a minivan, to contemplate how it is you live alone yet don't know a thing about cooking or grocery shopping, and why those stray plurals—i.e., "We went skiing this weekend"—keep meandering into your conversation.

Strong values that differ from the norm. I have been a single woman in Manhattan for more decades than I'm willing to admit, and I was sure I had seen everything until I signed-on to the internet. Suddenly I was receiving e-mail from a dazzling range of men with agendas, including polygamists, nudists, religious zealots of every denomination and, of course, a few convicts.

I am a live-and-let-live sort of person. (A good flirt is always open-minded.) But proclivities like these are deal-breaker issues. Nevertheless, if you have them, you *must* be up-front about them. Oh, you'll lose a few dates, for sure. Men and women like me will always hold out for a date who appreciates it when we dress for dinner, when we marry one person at a time, or arrange our conjugal visits somewhere where razor wire is not considered an interior design element. But it's your only chance of finding someone who shares your particular perspective on life.

Geography. I was visiting with my friend Robin when I happened upon her cleaning out her e-mail. Although she carefully scanned every response to the personal ad she had recently posted on a mountain biking board, she was systematically tossing letters from anyone who lived more than 500 miles away. When I asked her about it, she nodded with genuine chagrin. "It's a waste, I know. But geography is destiny. Long-distance love doesn't work. At least, not for me."

I had to agree. Though it's a smaller-than-ever world, geography *is* destiny. You simply cannot know a person you cannot see. And even a face-to-face meeting (or two) with a far-away partner does nothing to dispel any fantasies you may be harboring about him or her.

A relationship isn't real until it exists in the real world. Unless you live close to a cyberfriend or can visit often, your relationship is unlikely to develop, progress or succeed. My advice to you is that you stay in contact but don't romanticize the friendship. It will only make the inevitable more painful.

Not all of the input that causes on-line romances to crash comes from external sources. If, for example, you *can* take your friendship off-line but are reluctant to do so, if you seem to be getting so much more from your internet relationships than you do from off-line friends and co-workers, an all-too-common malady may be short-circuiting your chances for love.

ARE YOU A CYBER-ADDICT?

If you are, you're in good company—and plenty of it. Unfortunately, many shy or socially challenged singles have chosen to "live" in cyberspace rather than venture out into real space to meet face to face. Articles have appeared in psychological journals and newspapers indicating that more than a few World Wide Web users have crossed the boundary between aficionado and addict. But perhaps most surprising is the evidence that those who are most susceptible to the small screen's allure aren't science nerds or computer geeks. According to *Health* magazine, housewives, construction workers and secretaries most often fit the criteria for internet addiction. Once "wired," these individuals spend an average of thirty-eight hours each week (the equivalent of a full-time job) puttering on the 'net.

It is easy to see how that might happen. In the first weeks after signing-on, I was "welcomed" by the canned voice on my internet server more often than I was by any of my real-life friends. And so were most of the curious, intelligent and robustly functional men and women I have spoken to in the course of compiling this book. The World Wide Web is, after all, an alternate universe and your computer is your own personal portal to it. Having a direct path to such a wondrous place and then never passing through it is like building a rocket but never blasting off. The difference is that while most of us can take the information and conveniences the web offers and integrate them into our real lives, others among us become totally lost in cyberspace, absorbed by the web socially, sexually and intellectually.

Now that most servers are operating on a flat-fee basis, it has become less likely that you will go broke because of cyberaddiction. But that doesn't mean you won't pay dearly to join the virtual broken-hearts club. Cyber-addiction undermines marriages, destroys careers, erodes family life and obliterates friendships. Most of all, because internet addiction so often involves taking on alternate identities, role playing or other sexual or social situations involving an alter-ego that somehow feels "more like you," it makes playful, honest cyberflirtation without serious intent virtually impossible.

Are you caught in the 'net? If any of the following warning signs ring true to you, you may be.

1. Your friends, family members or co-workers complain that you spend too much time on the web. They feel you spend more time on-line than you do interacting with others face to face.

2. Your screen name seems more "like you" than your real name. Or you feel more vividly "yourself" on-line than you do among your real acquaintances.

3. When you can't sign-on, you can't bear to go on! Spend a few hours away from your computer and you are obsessing about who might be signed-on, whether you have mail, what you are missing, and the like.

4. When you sign-on after an absence, you experience a distinct sense of relief.

5. You have lost track of time on the 'net.

6. You have gotten out of bed in the middle of the night, skipped a social engagement or failed to fulfill a family obligation just so you could sign-on.

7. You feel more free to express yourself—sexually or socially— on the 'net. There are people on the internet who know things about you that no one else knows.

8. You check your e-mail more than five times each day.

9. You have logged on at work, at friend's houses, or at other inappropriate times.

10. You are defensive about the amount of time you spend on the 'net. The implication that you might be addicted sets you on edge.

Though some users and professionals pooh-pooh the idea of cyber-addiction (one of my former best friends is an addict who uses professional literature to argue that this condition simply does not exist), internet addiction is real. It has become such a problem in the workplace that many companies are offering the same types of rehabilitative services to their computer-addicted employees as they do for alcoholic and drug dependent personnel.

If you suspect you have a problem, you might check out a few of the on-line resources for additional information. (Try http://netad-diction.com/index.html.) But if you are looking for help, I suggest that you opt for face-to-face therapy. The last thing you need is counseling by computer.

HEARING AND HANDLING THE "N" WORD

If the other flirts in my seminar were jotting a few notes, Marci was writing an epic! While the rest of the class chatted and laughed and related their on-line flirting stories, Marci sat with her head down, her nose nearly touching the page of her notebook. Her pen moved continuously.

Finally, when I couldn't stand the mystery any longer, I approached Marci. "What on earth are you writing there?"

"I'm rewriting my profile," she answered, never taking her eyes off the page.

I hadn't known Marci before the seminar, but Marci was the type of woman you didn't have to know to recognize that she was a regular firebrand. Her profile *had* to be as memorable as she was.

"Whatever for?" I asked her.

Marci laid her notebook aside. "A week ago I had a wonderful chat with a man I met in my college's alumni chat room," she reported. "We really hit it off. In fact, we chatted for nearly two hours! Before we logged off, he promised he'd e-mail this week, but so far, I haven't heard from him." Marci sighed. "The chat was a great success, but something has obviously turned him off. I decided it must be my profile."

I didn't waste a minute. I immediately launched into what my friends laughingly call "Susan's 10-Minute Rejection Harangue." First I pointed out to Marci and the rest of the class that perfectly wonderful men and women are rejected every day and in every possible way—on subways and on-line, by phone, mail or modem.

Then I explained that rejection was rarely the result of anything we've done or said or failed to do as flirts. I told Marci and her classmates that we have a greater chance of being rejected because of someone's bad mood or lousy attitude or unfortunate haircut than we do because we don't, in some way, cut the mustard. Finally, to bring home my point, I related the story of the time I was flatly rejected—in full view of a room full of singles—by a man I'd asked to dance. The man explained to me later that he had just pulled in after a long, treacherous drive on the parkway and simply wanted to relax instead of socializing. In other words, he hadn't rejected me at all: He had merely rejected the opportunity to dance. Wouldn't that message be reassuring to Marci?

I would never know. Marci wasn't making eye contact with me. She was too busy scribbling in her notebook.

"What are you writing now?" I asked her.

"After I heard your story, I decided the profile probably wasn't the problem after all," Marci admitted. "So now I'm making a list of new screen names!"

I know it can be difficult to take rejection any way but personally, particularly for singles. While married people can always blame each other for their travails, we singles have learned to take the rap ourselves. If we are rejected, it isn't because of a tragic lack of judgment on the rejector's part. It's our hair (too thick) or our wallets (too thin) or our cars (too fast) or our "moves" (also too fast). And if some wishy-washy will o' the wisp we hardly know decides he or she doesn't like us or that he or she likes us too much, we don't blame it on his or her fickle nature. We blame ourselves for sending mixed signals or for sending clear messages that might have frightened him or her off, for being too "hovering" or too distant, for choosing such a cabbage head or allowing such a cabbage head to choose us. On bad days, we blame ourselves for being single. On good days we blame ourselves for even considering marriage.

There are a few factors that make rejection on the World Wide Web a bit easier to take. For one thing, you are never given the boot face to face, thus minimizing the personal embarassment factor. And, for the most part, any rejection you are likely to encounter is of an impersonal, almost clerical sort. Will your life careen into a tailspin because someone you hardly know has chosen to ignore your e-mail? Hardly.

Still, rejection can smart—unless you're smart enough to have adopted a philosophy of rejection. And what constitutes a philosophy of rejection? A few simple rationalizations (reasons or excuses why someone rejected you) or projections (ways to deflect the blame for the rejection back onto the person who rejected you) that make it possible for you to get over a friendship that's going nowhere, and get on with the fun and excitement of cyberflirtation!

What positive messages can you send yourself to turn those social setbacks into opportunities to move forward? These are the positive philosophical messages that work for me:

Cyber-rejection isn't personal. How can it be? Flirts like you may be one in a million, but your e-mail might still be passed up simply because it's one of a thousand. And about those discernment-challenged men and women who turn up their noses at your clever IMs or lively chat . . . they don't even know you! These and any other slights that come your way aren't based upon some flaw in *you;* they are based upon the questionable perceptions and unknown motivations of a perfect stranger. Now, I don't know about you, but I don't put much stock in the opinions of people I don't know. (I learned that by frequenting Yankee Stadium.) And I don't waste my time playing guessing games about what's really on other people's minds. (I learned that by watching the Amazing Kreskin.) All I know is, my 'net-quaintances are virtual unknowns to me. And people who don't know me cannot possibly reject *me.*

E-jection is not serious. Remember: The joy of cyberflirtation à la Rabin is that it enables you to explore the universe of available men and women *without serious intent.* But if socializing on the web leaves you feeling hurt, disappointed, angry, frustrated or desperate, if you feel increasingly pressured to find a partner or begin a meaningful relationship, your unspoken intentions may be overshadowing what should be playful interactions.

Try this. Rather than pin your hopes on a single prospect, try the structured mingling technique I describe on page 69. Choose a chat. Set a clock. Then move from prospect to prospect, exchanging niceties and ultimately e-mail addresses with as many conversational partners as you possibly can in the time you have allotted.

And if you happen to find a conversationalist who makes bells ring? First, check for an instant message. (There are bells, and there are *bells*.) Then ask that fascinating stranger if you can add him to your buddy list or e-mail her later, and *move along*. The reason flirting has cost you so much emotionally is because you have been investing too much in the people you meet. Better to reserve your assets for a relationship that pays *mutual* interest.

By the way, this is not only a terrific way to wean yourself off of the irrational (and disappointing) "this-could-be-the-one" belief system, it is also a sure-fire method for meeting masses of new people. And I've found no better cure for a slightly trampled heart than *lots* of good company.

Rejection is not the end of the world. Laura was a shy flirt whose chronic tendency to become tongue-tied made it nearly impossible for her to relate to the men she met in real life. Rather than urge her to confront her fears in a face-to-face milieu, I introduced her to the internet, hoping that on-line success might bolster Laura's off-line skills. Instead, there she sat, her glazed eyes glued to the chat log, her hands poised above the keyboard . . . totally "type-tied."

I asked Laura what was wrong.

"I simply don't know what to do! I mean, what do I say, Susan? What could I possibly say that would be more interesting to these people than what is already being said? And what if I offend somebody? Not that I would ever intend to, but . . ."

When Laura was through with her kvetch, I asked her to look over the chat log again. Was there anything so fascinating about the comments others had made? There was not. That's because, when your intention is breaking the ice, nearly any inane remark will do. Since there is nothing more inane than the ubiquitous age/sex/location checks, I urged Laura to jump right in and post her stats.

Just for the record, I have been exposed to dozens of age/location checks before. I have seen people comment on towns that are so small Rand McNally couldn't find them with a compass. I have seen people bond because they were the same age. But nobody was commenting on Laura's stats (f/33/NYC) though we waited. And waited.

"What's going on?" Laura asked finally.

I hemmed and hawed.

"I've been dissed, haven't I? Nobody's interested in me, are they?" she demanded.

I had to admit it—though Laura had served herself up like an hors d'oeuvre, there were no takers. I explained to Laura that there was no accounting for taste. I told her that some chat rooms could be rather inbred and "clubby" places. I begged her not to give up on the internet flirtation. Then, I noticed . . . Laura wasn't paying me any more attention than the chat participants had paid her. She was too busy typing!

I was incredulous! How did she transform herself from a chat room wallflower to the life of the party in only a matter of seconds?

"I just figured that if ignoring me is the worst they can do to me, I'll just say what I want," Laura observed, tapping out her thoughts on the latest political scandal brewing in Washington, D.C.

I'm pleased to tell you that Laura is now an accomplished internet flirt, and quite a fine face-to-face one, as well. But, most important, her story underscores one of the main precepts in my philosophy of rejection: Rejection is not the end of the world. It is survivable, overcomeable and, most of all, *instructional*. Go through it once and you discover that it isn't as bad as you imagined it would be. Move beyond it and you learn that rejection isn't the end of anything at all—it's the beginning of a fearless, freeing, incredibly rewarding and just-about-rejection-proof era of flirting.

Which brings us to the final, and possibly the most important, truth about rejection.

Rejection is a favor! Sure, rejection stings—particularly at point-blank range. But look at the bright side. That cyberjerk who dumps you before he's ever gotten to know you won't ever get a chance to convince you to remove your personal ad from the singles site ("Now that we've found each other, baby, what more could there be to look for?") while he responds to twenty more. And the "neurosurgeon" with the intriguing screen name ("Of course, Pandora is my only screen name. You mean, you can have more than one?") who relegates you to her permanent waiting room will only spare you the weeks of research it will take to determine that she is a fraud—and that the only surgery she routinely performs is the separation of the gullible from large sums of money.

Disappointments, turndowns and even putdowns are a part of life. But with a positive philosophy of rejection, you simply won't have time to obsess about the one who got away. You'll be too busy loading your data banks with the screen names and e-mail addresses of more compatible new friends.

DOWNLOADING MR./MS. WRONG

Most of the time, cyberflirting is an easy-come, easy-go kind of game. Companionship is simple to come by, and weeding out those who don't make it into the "increased intimacy round" can usually be accomplished with a polite, "I'm glad I met you. See you around the World Landmarks trivia game site sometime." Unfortunately, there are also those internet acquaintances who won't take no for an answer, who haunt you like a virus, infecting your attempts to flirt with others.

A former co-worker, Jim, recently encountered just such a person. At first Lola ("LolaPopXXX") seemed like a breath of fresh air—exhuberant, open-minded, fun—and, like Jim, looking for commitment. Indeed, the couple had "an arrangement." Both had agreed to stop looking for potential partners on-line, at least until they had fulfilled their plans to meet in a city midway between their respective homes. But when Jim became suspicious that Lola might still be on the lookout for a man with a more impressive profile than his own, he decided to test Lola's veracity. He adopted a new screen name, composed a profile that would make Donald Trump look like a slacker, and headed for a chat Lola was known to frequent. Sure enough, she was there. And she was falling all over her keyboard to charm the intriguing newcomer! Was she available? Jim asked. As a matter of fact, she was, Lola exclaimed. Did she like golf? (She'd told Jim that she hated the sport.) She loved it, she enthused. Could he have her phone number? Why certainly, Lola offered, passing along the private number it had taken the real Jim weeks to get.

Not wanting to waste another minute or virtual greeting card on an imposter, Jim sent Lola an e-mail explaining what he had done.

In it, he observed that since Lola had not removed herself from the singles market, she had obviously not found her heart's desire in him. He suggested that they remain friends but look elsewhere for a deeper connection.

But Lola was not to be deterred. She filled Jim's e-mail box with justifications for her behavior. When those failed, she flamed him repeatedly. When she got no response, she used the locator feature to hunt Jim down in the chats. There, she told lies about Jim and insulted him in a public forum. That was the final straw. Jim logged-off of the 'net and swore off cyberflirtation forever.

In chapter 4 I suggested that you create a special screen name just for flirting. It is probably becoming clear why I made that suggestion. Though "fatal attraction" flirts—or even benign but persistent ones—are few and far between, you may be forced to change your screen name in order to throw them off your trail. Since changing a professional screen name can jeopardize the flow of business and switching a personal one can cause havoc with messages from family and close friends, it is best to maintain an indentity you can slip into and out of with ease. You can always revert to your previous incarnation once the heat is off.

Once your name is changed, you may decide to alter your profile, as well. Profiles can be searched by keyword. A disgruntled ex who knows of your love for candlepin bowling or your weakness for Sidney Sheldon novels can hunt you down by your hobby. Either edit your profile or opt to do without. (Though you might bear in mind that some cyberflirts find people without profiles to be suspect.)

You might also keep your distance from your old haunts, particularly those your ex knows you frequent. Take a couple of weeks and try out some new chats. Or switch from chats to an on-line dating service. Just because a former friend claims to feel miserable and lonely, there's no sense in joining him.

If worse comes to worst, and you are being flamed, slandered, harassed, cursed out, or if you have received a message that contains either a material or an implied threat, copy the text in question and paste it into an e-mail addressed to the sender's server immediately. These behaviors constitute terms of service violations (some are also criminal offenses) and the server will likely take them very seriously. Your former friend may receive a stern warning or her internet service may be suspended altogether. One way or the other, your next IM will undoubtedly be more pleasant, and it isn't likely to be from her.

CYBERFLIRTING IS A NUMBERS GAME

That means getting over minor disappointments and getting on with the fun of flirting! These tips can help.

• If you're feeling rejected, take a deep breath, throw back your head and shout out my favorite four-letter word: Next! There are plenty more prospects where the last one came from. It's easier and faster than bar hopping; the next person is just a click away.
• Don't waste energy on blame or negative self-talk. Say something positive . . . to a new friend in the singles chats!
• Every minute you spend pondering someone's hidden motives or secret thoughts is a minute you aren't using to meet someone more compatible. If you find yourself worrying about what went wrong, fill in this sentence: "I'm glad he/she said no because _____." Then start looking for Mr. or Ms. Right!
• If you think for a moment that because you are a gregarious flirt you are immune to cyber-addiction, you are wrong. According to researchers, outgoing types are more prone to 'net-aholism than their shy counterparts. Why? Because they find it easier to build an alternative social network on the web.
• Just because you've given up on one inappropriate cyber-romance, that's no reason to give up on internet flirtation as a whole. It's hard enough to find true love without eliminating the biggest and most diverse hunting ground of all!

(For tips on navigating that "hunting ground," see the next chapter.)

9
Great Places to Meet People on the World Wide Web

A knowledgeable flirt like you knows exactly where to go looking for love in your neighborhood or in your city, but where do you begin to find close encounters of the romantic kind on the World Wide Web? Right here! Although this list of chats, personals sites and just-for-fun spots for singles of all ages is by no means exhaustive, and websites are expanding and changing daily, it should give you plenty of ideas for flirting forums that suit your style, geographical realities and personal preferences.

A note, however: There is a specialized site or forum somewhere on the internet where you can explore just about any interest you may have—no matter how far beyond the fringe that activity might seem. If you have such an agenda, I suggest that you seek out the appropriate forum and address it there rather than advertising it on message boards or in public chat rooms. You'll have better luck if you target your message to the most responsive audience, and you'll spare yourself a lot of unpleasant e-mail from those who don't understand or wish to transform you.

SEARCH ENGINES

An easy-to-use search engine makes it quick and efficient to gather information on any subject. It also provides the cyberflirt with an instantaneous link to the tens of thousands of like-minded men and women who share his or her hobbies and interests.

Since every search engine presents and categorizes its information differently, I suggest that you try a few and then decide which works best for you.

To get started, type in the keywords "singles," "romance" or "dating."

Yahoo:
   http://www.yahoo.com/
Lycos:
   http://www.lycos.com/
Altavista:
   http://www.altavista.com/
Webcrawler:
   http://www.webcrawler.com/
Excite:
   http://www.excite.com/
Infoseek:
   http://www.infoseek.com/

And here's a particularly charming one to try (It even asks you to phrase your question in "plain English"!):

Jeeves
   http://www.askjeeves.com/

MUST-SEE SITES FOR SINGLES

Cupid's Network bills itself as "the world's largest network of romantic eligibles on the Internet" and I have no reason to doubt that claim. A true "supersite" directory encompassing more than 1500 separate websites specifically designed for singles, Cupid's

Network features a national calendar of singles events, a comprehensive listing of books, audiotapes and videotapes of interest to singles, a million personal ads to browse at your convenience (Nobody out there? Ha!) and links to a broad range of singles resources including magazines, organizations, dating and matchmaking services and other lifestyle-related sites too numerous to mention. Cupid's Network gets over one million "hits" per day. There is no fee.

http://www.cupidnet.com/

American Singles is the largest nonprofit dating service with over 200,000 members worldwide. This service is very easy to use and designed with simplicity in mind, which probably explains its popularity. The profiles are conveniently arranged by location. American Singles offers its members several communications options including: e-mail (simply click on the e-mail icon under a member's profile), "snail mail" forwarding (a wonderful option for those who prefer to exchange "real" letters but don't want to give our their home address) and an active chat area. You'll also find a large list of "HappyEndings" where former members describe their experiences of meeting someone on-line—fun reading. The service is basically free, although donations are appreciated to cover costs. There are also a few low-cost "value-added" services that make this one of the most useful sites around.

http://www.as.org/

Match.com is a very comprehensive and professionally run, popular matchmaking site with over 100,000 members. It offers an easy-to-use computer matching tool that lets you narrow down prospects. It also provides its members the opportunity to create a "screen name" they can use for flirting purposes so they can e-mail in confidence without ever revealing their true identities.

They also have an active chat area, special events, an on-line magazine and advice on love, sex, astrology, etc. They have a varied fee schedule.

http://www.match.com/

To me, Web Match has a nice, "homey" atmosphere and that may make it a must-see for cyberflirts who feel lost in a large crowd. A service that boasts 50,000 personals on file, Web Match also offers scheduled chats, an e-postcard exchange (I love e-postcards!) and even an advice feature ("Ask Darlene"). Shy or "I-Don't-Flirt" Flirts who still need coaxing might enjoying browsing the love stories and testimonials.

Inspirational!

http://www.webmatch.com/

SPECIAL INTERESTS

You will find a great many links to special interest sites on any of the "supersites" such as Cupid's Network. In addition, you might try these.

http://www.singlesalley.com/ Personals for people with adventurous lifestyles.

http://www.cartalk.com/ Are you an elegant vintage Mercedes sedan or are you more of a fast-and-jazzy IROC-type? On this amusing website, well-engineered eligibles describe themselves as cars!

http://www.animalpeople.com/ Looking for a certain someone to share your love for your four-legged friends? Search here first.

http://www.christsingles.com/singles/ An international network of Christian singles that matches members by denomination and personal interests. There is a fee.

http://www.JewishPersonals.com/ or JSNNET.com/ is about the newspapers with Jewish personal ads.

http://www.latina.com/ The on-line version of *Latina* magazine. Chock-full of features including message boards, scheduled chats, gossip and entertainment items, briefs on issues of interest to Hispanic people and more.

http://www.citysearchNYC.com/ A great resource for on-line flirts looking for off-line love in NYC. You can check out other cities as well.

http://www.pwp.org/ Parents Without Partners homepage. Offers chats, pen pals and bulletins boards that could be invaluable to single parents.

http://www.webpersonals.com/ Free personal ads,

activities, pen pal lists for men seeking men, women seeking women.

http://www.flirts.com/ Advice site from the "Angel of Flirting" on kissing, being attractive and the married flirt— all of which could be helpful, but who is this Angel?

Sites of Interest to Seniors

http://www.aarp.org/ Homepage of the American Association of Retired Persons. While there are no chats or message boards per se, this is a great source of information on AARP-sponsored activities that can bring you into contact with that "special someone."

http://www.thirdage.com/ This upbeat, creative, funny, fascinating and hip site bills itself as "the web for adults." It's a virtual community dedicated to educating, entertaining and bringing together men and women who have reached their "third age." You'll find tons of information here on issues from health to finance, chats, regional links and a wonderful selection of scheduled forums on a wide variety of subjects from volunteerism to computer know-how to hot sex over fifty.

EXOTIC DESTINATIONS FOR A VIRTUAL DATE

The Smithsonian. This something-for-everyone site offers click-and-go links to each of the Smithsonian museums. You and a new friend might decide, for example, to take in the sights at the Hirshhorn Museum and Sculpture Garden. Or, if you're feeling more adventurous, you might opt for the National Zoo Audio Wand Tour. A real tour with complete audio accompaniment, this is the same tour you and your 'net friend would have rented had you visited the zoo in real life.

http://www.si.edu/

Art listings. Museums make great dates, and that holds true whether you're dating on-line or off. And this cultural clearinghouse allows you to choose your destination from among the world's best. With links to dozens of diverse museums from the Andy Warhol Museum in Pittsburgh to the Louvre, and simple-to-use scrollbars so you can select by state or country, there is truly something for everyone here.

http://www.artlistings.com/artlistings/museums/

The Metropolitan Museum of Art. When I want to cut to the chase and steep myself in a familiar yet always-evolving gallery, I go straight to the Metropolitan Museum of Art. Where else can I browse among armor and arms, Greek statuary, musical instruments and cat mummies all in one day? It's a true adventure, and you don't even have to get on the subway. I also love browsing in the gift shop.

http://www.metmuseum.org/

International Sites

Great Britain. Okay, I admit it: I'm a sucker for royalty. If you or your date share my fetish for crowned heads (And you very well might. After all, the royal family didn't become Britain's most popular tourist attraction by default!), run, don't walk, to this wonderful site. British sitcoms only last a half an hour, but here you can browse indefinitely, wallowing in history, drinking in the stories of the British monarchs both famous and infamous, touring the palaces (including the recent restoration of Windsor Castle) and inventorying the royal art collection. In short: It's just about everything worth seeing, excepting Charlie's ears.

http://www.royal.gov.uk/

Westminster Abbey. The only downer I experienced on a recent trip to London was that I didn't have the time to take in all the fascinating nooks and crannies of Westminster Abbey. This site more than makes up for the realities of closed-ended travel. I suggest that you take this tour with the first Anglophile you meet. Not only can you take in the tomb of Mary Queen of Scots and wax poetic in Poet's Corner, if you have installed a Real Audio feature you can even listen to the famed Westminster choir, the extraordinary organ and the tolling of the bells.

http://www.westminster-abbey.org/

Paris. What lovelier locale could there be for a first date than the City of Lights? Best of all, if there's a lull in the conversation, you can always virtual shop until you virtually drop.

http://www.paris.org/

The Sistine Chapel. The accuracy of the Sistine Chapel's recent restoration will be debated by art historians for years to come. But the chapel's complex beauty remains an indisputable fact. Here is one locale so magnificent and awe-inspiring, it is virtually impossible to suffer through an insufferable date. Enjoy!

http://www.christusrex.org/www/sistine/O-Sistine.html/

Mount Everest. Although this site is based on an expedition that took place more than a year ago, I find myself returning to it again and again. A particularly vivid and realistic site, this source allows me to experience (vicariously) Everest's power and allure, to see as if through my own eyes the staggeringly beautiful top-of-the-world vistas few people have seen (like the breathtaking and treacherous Icefall), and to come to know the danger, hardship and exhilaration of climbing to the top of the world's highest mountain. (Note: Men love this site!)

http://everest. mountainzone.com/

The Titanic. If you prefer to travel in comfort (bring your own lifeboat!), you and a date can zip back in time and tour the *Titanic* as she prepares to embark on her maiden voyage. Conversation flows like claret when you're exploring the grand staircase, the exceptionally ornate staterooms and the cushy Turkish baths with a convivial companion. But if you feel the need to rub shoulders with the hoi-polloi, you can always "meet" some of the swells who made the ship's first and last voyage so memorable. A fun tie-in to a current subject of interest.

http://www.ravens.net/titanic/

A musical interlude. Who wouldn't love to while away a laid-back first date listening to music together? Well, I'm happy to report that you can now share your favorite sounds with your favorite chat partner by visiting the CDnow site. If you have installed RealAudio on your computer, you can sample a wide range of CDs, critique them to each other and suggest those that tickle your fancy. You'll soon discover whether your musical taste is compatible or whether it's time to "rock on."

http://www.cdnow.com/

AOL SITES OF INTEREST

With over 12 million subscribers in the United States and abroad, America Online is now the largest internet service. It also offers more opportunities for cyberflirtation per square inch of screen than any one man or woman could possibly explore in a year. I know. I've tried. But every time I get close to exhausting the available sites, AOL adds a few more dishy options to the singles smorgasbord. Among the highlights are:

AstroMates. I know, it just isn't cool to ask someone's sign in a real-life bar, but you can let your interest in astrology out of the closet when you're searching for your soul mate at this heavenly site! With a photo gallery, profiles and chats in the Astro Lounge, this site is worth checking out even if Mars *is* in retrograde.
Keyword: AstroMates

Love@aol. A good all-around romance site with chats, free photo personals and tips for creating a dynamite ad, a newsletter, success stories, a daily love horoscope and the opportunity to "meet 50,000 people from your living room." Who could ask for anything more?
Keyword: love@aol

Christianity Online Singles Connection. If a believer is what you are looking for, this site may make a believer out of you. CO is an efficiently designed resource. Here chats are conveniently grouped by age and it is easy to read the most recently placed personals first. There are also games and contests and plenty of opportunity to develop your spirituality (in addition to your buddy list).
Keyword: CO

Jewish Singles. I've visited hundreds of singles sites but never have I seen such an interesting message board as the one at Jewish Singles! With categories that range from food and holidays to the Torah and science to arts and culture to religious issues, there is ample opportunity to meet like-minded—or simply interesting— new friends here. As if that isn't enough, Jewish Singles offers live chats and, of course, a matchmaking service that caters to every lifestyle from Orthodox/Orthodox unions to gay and lesbian romance.

Keyword: Jewish Singles

Passport to Love. A must-see for anyone who wants to make an international love-match. Passport to Love offers you the option of placing a picture personal, a large international database of profiles searchable by profession, region, religion or looks, live chats and a positively charming forum where you can share your country's love customs and perhaps pick up a few new ones as well.

Keyword: PPL

NetNoir. African-American flirts won't want to miss NetNoir, a lively locale for romance, information, and events of cultural interest. Featuring live chats, free e-mail, personals you can browse by sex, region, age and hobby and the "Black Boards" message boards, NetNoir comes complete with information on African-American weddings, just in case you and some lucky acquaintance really hit it off.

Keyword: NetNoir

As if that's not enough, you'll find more romantic alternatives on nearly every other channel on the AOL menu. Doubt me? Check out the AOL news on the News Channel (keyword: news). Not only can you vent your spleen on all manner of issues on the news message boards (thus reserving your sweeter self for flirtation) you can meet compatible "newsies" by participating in the scheduled chats. Or, if you're a movie, music or TV buff, opt for the Entertainment Channel. The Inner Circle chat room (keyword: inner circle) will put you in touch with other media junkies. If you still haven't found a spot that "clicks," head for Hobby Central on the Interests Channel. There you can scroll down a menu of twenty-eight pastimes, from antiquing to extreme sports to photography to writing, all with message boards where you can connect with eligible men and women who share your interests. Even the Games Channel has turned out to be a winner for me. Every time I play a game of Wipeout Trivia, I take a moment to congratulate the winner. Before I know it, I've broken the ice (and picked up some pointers). And I'm happy to say that I've met more honest, straightforward singles "playing games" than I've met at some social functions. Some of them will be on my buddy lists forever.

NICE THINGS TO SEND

Greeting cards. There are many free sites, including some tailored to specific hobbies, activities and collections. (Hallmark take note: Greetings just aren't greetings anymore unless they're animated and set to a toe-tapping melody!) But the site I find myself turning to again and again is:

http://www/bluemountain.com/

Virtual bouquets. Virtual flowers can be a pain to "pick up." (I'd gladly give a delivery man a tip rather than negotiate a 30-digit web address.) They can also make one long for the real thing. Nevertheless, you can stop and smell the virtual flowers at:

http://www.virtualflorist.com/ (You can even spend a few bucks and send the real thing!)

Anonymous love letters. Although I feel that no billet doux should ever go unsigned (what kind of a flirt composes a memorable missive then doesn't stick around to take the credit?), you may want to hide your identity but not your feelings. Go to the main menu at: http://www.lovelife.com/

Virtual balloon bouquets. High hopes for that on-line romance? Send him or her a balloon arrangement! Type in:

http://www.bizshoppe.com/balloon/index.html

A virtual vacation. To impress a stressed-out flirt, a virtual vacation might be just the ticket:

http://www.virtual-vacation.com/index.shtml

Instant anagrams. It can be lots of fun to see what anagrams can be made from the letters in a new friend's name. For instance, one anagram of my co-writer, Barbara Lagowski's, name is "A Barb gal is ok." But I prefer the anagram the finder came up with for my own monicker: "Brain Susan." Just make sure the anagram you send is complimentary. Try: http://www.anagramfinder.com/

SOME ADVICE ON ADVICE

You'll find advice, romance and self-help sites all over the internet and on many server-supported sites. Because I have found some of the guidance on these sites to be questionable—and on occasion, even dangerous—I am not recommending any of them.

The internet may be the last of a breed: It is truly a free-speech forum. It does not censor. Anyone with iffy or even nonexistent credentials can hang out an http and set up a homepage. Therefore, it is up to you, the consumer, to decide how credible these advisors are and whether you should take or leave their recommendations. Use your judgment. Ask yourself whether the guidance rings true. Take the time to bone up on an advisor's biographical and professional background. Does he have a proven track record? Is she well known as a professional? In this instance, it's best to choose a person "with a past." A background can be traced, while credentials are sometimes fictitious.

Most of all, make sure any advice you're taking is safe. If you are in doubt, reread my tips for safe internet flirting on page 6. Although my rules are considerably more conservative than those offered by other advice gurus, it is safer to do things my way when you're traveling the information highway.

Epilogue

Why did I choose to write about flirting, dating and mating on the internet? The answer is simple. I owe my loyal readership, and all singles not yet acquainted with my philosophy of flirting and fun, a trip to the largest and most exciting meeting place for singles to mix and mingle in the world—cyberspace! It is a party that never ends, which we can access whenever we wish, without ever leaving our homes. *Cyberflirt* teaches you the tips and techniques to travel an avenue bigger and better than you could ever imagine—reaching from small town America to the Great Wall of China. It is the "great white way" to singles as Broadway is to the actor.

That is not to say the internet is "It"—the final frontier for flirting. No way. I could not be true to my philosophy if I did not remind you to still go out and flirt, everywhere, every time you have a chance, as I do. Life is meant to be adventure: in town, out of town and in cyberspace. But for those cold winter nights, the evenings you're just too tired to attend a lecture at the library, have a nasty cold or are catching up on business reading and need to take a short break, I say, go to the internet. If, at times, you feel you've been there, done that and need a new milieu, go to the internet. You have no time, you're not in the mood to put on makeup, a shirt and tie, go to the internet. You can cyberflirt any time, all day and more, if you cross time zones. Negotiating the 'net is the most all-engrossing, challenging singles party of the nineties and will take you into the millenium.

It is important to me to bring this definitive guide for a safe, smart social life for savvy singles to everyone trying to meet that special someone, to make friends or to just have fun. I've had a ball and met great people whom I never would have had the time or opportunity to meet without this medium. I wish this for all of you.

Cyberspace makes the song true—it *is* a small world after all, full of fascinating people to explore. Don't let the naysayers and negative press prevent you from exploring this great social scene. Start with some of my suggestions and then be creative. Cyberspace is limitless. It's a place to be inventive; to let out the child in you. Be playful and polite, and success is guaranteed. Take the risk, flirt, date and meet your mate with this book as your guide to smart and safe fun. Happy cyberflirting!

AUTHOR'S NOTE

Susan Rabin hopes *Cyberflirt* has opened a new world of fun, friends and flirting for you! If you are interested in purchasing her audiocassettes, videocassette or props, go to her website: www.schoolofflirting.com or send a check or money order (postage included) for the items below to:

Susan Rabin CF
P.O. Box 660
New York, NY 10028

Videocassette, *How to Flirt, Date and Meet Your Mate*, $19
Audiocassettes, *How to Flirt, Date and Meet Your Mate*, $14
    How to Read a Man/Woman Like a Book, $14
    How to Deal with Difficult People, $14
    (Any two cassettes $25; three cassettes $39)
Flirting props *(to give that other "someone" a reason to talk to you)*
    Flashing Flirting Ring $6
    Flirting T-Shirt $12
    Flirting Hat $12
    Nicebreaker® Meeting Cards $9

Susan Rabin's books, *How to Attract Anyone, Anytime, Anyplace* and *101 Ways to Flirt*, are available in bookstores everywhere and can be found on the web at Amazon.com, Borders.com and BarnesandNoble.com, or call Penguin Putnam at (800) 253-6476.